THE SEV
FOR A LIFETIME OF LOVE AND COMPANIONSHIP

Everyone enters a marriage with expectations: some vague, some specific; some romantic, some pragmatic. . . . Companionship and financial security. Happiness and status. Love and fidelity. As time and life go on, a growing relationship reveals to you truths about yourself and what really makes you—and your spouse—happy. Soon your mate's happiness becomes as important to you as your own, and the pleasure of giving surpasses that of getting.

None of this happens suddenly. It's a progression that moves along gradually from one level to the next.

This book is about those levels. It's about expectations and reconciliations and happy marriage. I believe that everyone entering a marital relationship or already in one can be helped immeasurably by knowing that there are predictable stages that are natural, even necessary, to the growth and development of a good mariage.

Also by Cynthia S. Smith

DOCTORS' WIVES: The Truth about Medical Marriages

STEP-BY-STEP ADVERTISING

THE SEVEN LEVELS OF MARRIAGE

Expectations Vs. Reality

by Cynthia S. Smith

IVY BOOKS • NEW YORK

Ivy Books
Published by Ballantine Books

Library of Congress Catalog Card Number: 86-19143

ISBN 0-8041-0152-3

This edition published by arrangement with Lyle Stuart Inc.

Manufactured in the United States of America

First Ivy Books Edition: January 1988

To David and treasured memories

Contents

3. Parenthood? 61

The "yes" or "no" decision. Do I/you/we really want children? When is the "right time" and how about that biological clock? Do I want to put my career on hold (her)? Tangible drawbacks vs. intangible benefits. Will it be worth it and how do we know? Parental and societal pressure. How couples make choices.

4. Family 81

The birth and afterbirth. His jealousy over divided attention and affection. Time sharing and his anger over loss of services (sexual and other). The pleasure and pride. The new lineup—and now we are three. The growing family and growing responsibilities. Late-working fathers and resentful wives ("If you really cared, you'd be home on time"). The double load of the working mother. Disputes over child-rearing.

5. R&R (Rebirth [hers] and Reconciliation [his]) 111

"I'm free, now it's time for me," says she. Re-entry into the career world. The exhilaration of her new self-gratifying life. Adjusting his dreams downward: The world I didn't conquer. Male mid-life crisis. Lousy sex and fears of impotence. Role reversal and reverse penis envy. Is she dominant and who cares so long as it works. Reaction of children to the new lineup.

6. Hum-Drum 139

The bane of boredom and the dangers of dalliance. The "I need space" cliché and other excuses for having affairs. The youth mania: Grecian Formula and cosmetic surgery. Macho and mortality: "They're dropping like flies." A return to Me-ism. The Gauguin syndrome and other unrealistic fantasies.

7. Freedom 157

The kids are gone—we're back to just us. Wonderful total freedom from responsibility. The pleasures of coitus non interruptus. New sybaritic lifestyle: sunshine, security and seeing the world. The problem of the returning child: the guilt of saying, "No, you can't come home again. We served our time . . . now we want to enjoy being just us." Retirement and dealing with 24-hours-a-day togetherness. When he retires and she doesn't. In sickness and in health. The fulfilling rewards of a lifetime together.

Bibliography 195

Expectations

Blessed be he who expects nothing for he shall never be disappointed.

—Alexander Pope

"We're both executives, for God's sake. Why do I do the cooking and cleanup while he sips martinis in front of the TV?"

"He wanted children as much as I did. So how come I'm the one who changes diapers, feeds and bathes the baby while he just plays with her? It's not fair!"

"Sure I understand when he loses a big deal and his ego is battered, I'm supposed to tiptoe around the house and minister to his psyche. Then how come when I lose a case and come home beat, he doesn't want to hear about it? Shouldn't I be entitled to equal treatment?"

"Not *fair*." "I'm *entitled*." It's the recurrent theme that threads through discussions I held with young married women who grew up in the Sixties and married in the Seventies and Eighties. Obviously no one told them that nowhere is it written that life is meant to be fair and there are no implicit entitlements. The reality is that a successful marriage is not a legally drawn-up business arrangement where both sides must spell out who does what in order to get what and that the parties of the first and second parts do not necessarily emerge with parity. The fact is that marriages only work well when both sides desist from keeping scorecards of each other's performance and contributions to their coexistence.

But today we are dealing with the young woman who has been educated to fulfill every ounce of her potential and to be anything she wants to be, no holds barred. She is told in books, newspaper and magazine articles that she is equal to men. And even in the primal arena for emotional development, the home, fathers who used to boast only of the achievements of their sons now speak with pride and wonder of their daughters, the doctor or lawyer, and look upon their sons' pursuits as commonplace. In the woman-aware era of ERA, women are the stars and men's rights are going the way of WASPS' rights. Women are feeling their oats. They are heading into the world with great expectations of leading full unconstrained lives combining the emotional fulfillments of marriage and parenthood plus the ego and economic satisfactions of careers. And they are suffering disillusionment, dissatisfaction and painful disappointments.

For with whom must they share this perfect world? Regard the young man who grew up in the Sixties and reached so-called manhood in the Seventies and Eighties. This darling grew up under the old regime—prince of the family, lovingly tended by Mom and promised the privileges of "a man's world" by Dad. Suddenly in the Seventies when he should start reaping the pledged pleasures of the male ascendency and the unquestioning subordinate role of women, the rules changed. What used to be accepted as givens, he now has to fight to earn. He enters a work force where competent women are competitive contenders. He enters a social scene where women, instead of waiting demurely to be wooed, impose standards on his sexual performance. He encounters role reversals in relationships wherein women now openly evince the assertiveness and agressiveness that their mothers were taught to conceal in order to avoid threats to the fragile male ego ("Don't let him see how smart you are or you'll never get a husband"). All his life he had expectations of settling down with a wife who would regard him as the master and provider of the home and would do her share by supplying him with love, respect, creature comforts and bringing up his children. Instead he's faced with women who have been made aware that they now have choices—they too are entitled to succor and indulgence and they do not have to be totally responsible for raising the children. In fact, they are even permitted to not have children at all if they so opt. How does this confused young man cope with the change in roles and thwarting of his expectations? Not well.

When I interviewed a charming woman who had been married for fifty years and asked her the secret of a successful marriage, she had it in one word "Overlooking." "I overlooked a lot. . . . he overlooked a lot. We got along."

That was fifty years ago. But now we're faced with men and women who are fighting to understand their own identities . . . who are constantly searching their psyches to figure out why they do what they do—and to be continually on guard against those who are trying to do unto them. This nonsense jargon of "I need space" and "I don't want to get involved" is the language of fear . . . dreadful apprehension that yielding will in some way diminish them. They are so unsure of their societal positions that they seek for signs of personal danger in all relationships. Even liking someone too much becomes a threat. "If I become too attached to her, then what will become of *me*"? There's always that abiding concern with *me*.

Today, we have young men and women who are fighting fiercely to hold on to their so-called freedom and individuality and in doing so have created their own personal prisons. Accommodation, compromise, overlooking, giving in—the true language of love and marriage—is an anathema to them. What's worse is they do not even understand the reasons for this sort of behavior. The "Why should I?" attitude is antithetical to a successful marriage.

Yet the marriage rate is increasing. But unfortunately, so is the divorce rate. Perhaps the biggest reason for failed marriages is unrealistic expectations.

According to *Husbands and Wives: A Nationwide Survey of Marriage** done in 1979 by Dr. Anthony Pietropinto and Jacqueline Simenauer, who surveyed 4,000 marriages, "What we clearly see emerging is a set of assumptions about modern marriage that run contradictory to our traditional expectations. If expectations have changed and marriage has not, our problem may be that we, like Lewis Carroll's White Knight, 'madly squeeze a right-hand foot into a left-hand shoe' and are feeling the pinch."

Marriage is a very volatile business; it changes its configuration as times change and people change. And the ability to accommodate to the changes that occur within ourselves and our mates is the key to a successful marital partnership.

Everyone entering marriage is innundated with these same caveats and advice. "Compromise." "Give

*New York: Times Books, 1979.

in." I remember hearing those words of wisdom over and over again from well-meaning relatives just before my wedding. Female relatives, of course. Men never thought about accommodation or consideration. I also recall being somewhat puzzled and frightened by these warnings.

Overlook what? Accommodate what? What things should I expect him to do that I would have to overlook? What conflicts would I expect to occur that would demand my compromise? What sort of erratic behavior would take place that would require my accommodation? If only someone had prepared me for the realities I would encounter along the way instead of issuing vague exhortations, life would have been lots easier. Now as I look back (I was married to the same man for 34 years) I see marriage as a movable feast . . . it goes through stages—levels that we must pass through. And as I began to review the successful marriages of various friends, I perceived patterns of similarity in the phases we all encountered and endured.

Everyone enters a marriage with a series of expectations. Some vague, some specific. Some romantic, some pragmatic. Like companionship and financial security. Happiness and status. Love and fidelity. The expectations involve what you plan to contribute to the arrangement and what you feel your spouse should supply. And then your marriage goes through periods of modifying your expectations to accommodate to the realities.

As you live together, changes take place in your perceptions of what you expected as against what you really care about and need. Priorities alter . . . traits you thought vitally important in a mate assume minor significance. Consciously and subconsciously, you may minimize elements of character you thought mandatory in a spouse, and appreciate the value of lovely qualities you had never considered. As time and life go on, a growing relationship reveals to you truths about yourself and what really makes you happy. And your spouse happy. Soon your mate's happiness becomes as important to you as your own because you love him/her and the pleasure of giving surpasses that of getting. Then the sense of compromising, the awareness of giving in—that evaporates and you are married.

None of this happens suddenly. You don't wake up one morning and announce "Today's the day I take the 'his' and 'hers' off the towels because we are now 'us.' " It's a progression of relationship that moves along gradually from one level to the next.

This book is about those levels. And expectations and reconciliations to reality. *And happy marriage.* Because I believe that everyone entering a marital relationship and everyone in one can be helped immeasurably by knowing that there are predictable stages that are natural, even necessary, to the growth and development of a good marriage.

I interviewed married men and women of all ages, geographic loci, socio-economic and educational strata. The questions covered expectations, feelings, occurrences and behavior sustained during different years of their marriages. The patterns of similarity in the chronology of their experiences dictated the formulation of the Seven Levels.

The attitudes of the couples I spoke to reaffirm that marriage is indeed a marvelously satisfying relationship, and that Noah and God knew what they were about when they insisted on two by twos. True, you have to bend a bit here and there and learn to reconcile your myths with reality and transmute your expectations, but it's worth it.

And it never just happens miraculously. What became evident to me is that successfully married couples valued the relationship and were willing to fight for its life. The dynamics of discovering one's own and each other's true self often involves tensions that can be tortuous. It helps to know that what you are experiencing is universal. What you may perceive as a unique and major problem in your marriage may be a common garden-variety difficulty encountered by all couples . . . the kind that is normal to your Level and can be worked out or merely will disappear in time.

It can be very comforting to learn that you are not alone in your unhappiness over specific disagreements that seem to be uniquely personal and irreconcilable. It is very reassuring to discover that other married people have gone through similar strife and emerged with the marriage intact, usually the stronger for having survived the struggle.

How I wish I had known all this before. How much easier my early married years could have been had I known that the initial sense of lonely separateness would pass. And to have realized that my husband's total withdrawal during our tenth year of marriage was not a rejection of me but merely a temporary condition that would pass after he fought and won the battles with his own dragons. Shakespeare in his "All the world's a stage" speech in *As You Like It* tells us that Man lives through seven stages. Erik Erikson charted a life cycle of eight stages each marked by a crisis. Gail Sheehy in her book *Passages* takes us through an adult life that must undergo a series of predictable and painful crises.

After discussions with many married couples, it became apparent to me that marriage has its own slower perhaps less dramatic tempo of development because it involves not one but three lives . . . his, hers and theirs. Changes take place at a more evolutionary pace since they come about as the result of not just one person's crisis but the familial interaction that ensues. What happens within him affects her . . . just as her inner growth struggles must influence him. And the responses and handling of each other's egocentric turmoil alters that living entity called Marriage. "If like Tennyson's Ulysses, we are a part of all that we have met, then we are part of our spouses; and if our partners change, then we are part of those changes, as they are part of ours."*

One partner may have a startling crisis, a life-altering epiphany. But there is of necessity a time lag that can be days, weeks, months even a year as the other partner becomes more aware that some change has occurred and then reacts, responds, fully absorbs the impact on their relationship and then finally accepts. It takes a long time for the Ping-Pong principle of human relations to do its work, wherein the problem is tossed back from one to the other. "That's how I am *now,* and if you can't handle it, then it's your problem." Countered by "Why should I have to cope with your sick behavior? You're the one who obviously needs a shrink." And then comes the soul-searching and the shifting of gears to accommodate to the new persona suddenly introduced into their established relationship that inevitably alters the shape of their marriage.

The time factor in the process varied with the participants plus the external factors in their lives. Some marriages move from Level to Level within months . . . some take two, three years. It's not

*Ibid.

based on time or age. It is a maturation and the time element is unimportant. The procedure may be stormy or silent, may include hysterical confrontations or just quiet anguish and acceptance. But if the marriage is solid, based on love, understanding, mutual respect and, above all, a deep desire to continue, then it will assimilate the new conditions and emerge with a reinforced relationship that will provide greater strength to make the next Level that much easier to handle.

The aim of this book is to provide not a marriage manual, but a guide to self-examination. To demystify the unknown and to prepare participants for what is to come. To offer the comfort of knowing that what you encounter is normalcy and not aberration. To provide the consolation of certainty that seemingly erratic conduct is not a sign of rejection or personal failure but merely natural human behavior. And most of all, it is to give every married person the strength of knowing that it continues to get better and better, and that the passing through each Level bonds the marriage into a marvelous, productive and soul-nourishing relationship that makes one appreciate its permanence as an institution. According to Masters and Johnson in their book *The Pleasure Bond,* "Marriage can become deeper and richer and more intense over a period of time as your commitment to each other becomes reinforced by all the experiences, good and bad, that you share."*

*Boston: Little Brown and Company, 1975.

THE FIRST LEVEL

Entry

(The Beginning)

It begins in delight and ends in wisdom.
—Robert Frost

Getting to Know You
Getting to Know Me

Ellen sat in bed and seethed as she looked down at her now blissfully sleeping husband who was thoroughly at peace after listening to the half-hour of calming encouragement given to him by his wonderfully supportive wife.

"What the hell's in this for me?" she fumed inwardly. "What do I need this bullshit for?"

It was the usual nighttime culmination of one of Tom's nothing-happened days which inevitably ended up with him lying in bed staring at the ceiling and going into one of his "I'm-a-failure-you-should-have-married-a-dentist" speeches. And as usual Ellen rose to the occasion with rah-rah rhetoric to soothe his despair. But after thirty minutes of reassurance about his talent, and how it's just a question of finding the right job, and the usual conclusion where Tom said lovingly, "You're marvelous . . . what would I do without you?" and then turned over and dropped off to sleep . . . Ellen was drained and furious.

"Sure you don't know what to do without me,"

she thought as she went to the bathroom to take a Valium. "But I sure as hell know what I'd do without you. I'd find a husband who would take care of *me*. And I'd find a husband whose sex drive didn't go into neutral every time he had a rough day."

Ellen and Tom were married seven months before in what one of their friends had called a "four alarm wedding." The traditional tuxedos and white lace, a sit-down dinner for one hundred and twenty, the entire affair had been a spectacle right out of the pages of *Modern Bride* magazine and was followed up with the quintessential Caribbean honeymoon. Ellen at age 25 was an assistant buyer for a large department store and was regarded as a rising star slated for either a major buying position or a spot in the corporate hierarchy. Highly intelligent and capable, she had the special insight and wisdom that enabled her to get the people she worked with to work for her, both at the subordinate and superior levels. It was just that strength that appealed to Tom. A handsome man of 29, he was a talented writer who had floundered for years with uncertain career goals and made his living in the precarious world of free-lancing. They met at a party to raise money for a political candidate whom neither supported but attended purely as a social function and were both struck simultaneously with what was known in the Rock Hudson-Doris Day films as "love at first sight." Ellen had suffered all her male-female-relationship days under the burdensome epithet of "strong and aggressive" which strong men found competitive and weak men found threatening. She had been brought up to believe that she needed to marry a powerful man who could dominate or at least cope with her agile mind. However, when she met Tom, she was instantly taken with his good looks, easy charm and openly delighted admiration for her dynamic personality. Within six months of spending every moment of their free time together, they decided to get married.

Actually Ellen had made up her mind within three months that this was the man she did not want to live without. The next three months were devoted to the usual female job of convincing the man to take the horrendous step of making a commitment.

One of womankind's greatest problems is the balk barrier to marriage, which resides in the fortunately reachable recesses of the male psyches, that makes them resist taking the Big Step. The picture of man on bended knee pleading with fair maiden for her hand in marriage is only for Whitman Sampler ads. These days men think of marriage strictly in the abstract.

"Sure, someday I want to marry somebody."

But which day and which body? In most cases, if it were not for the woman insisting on a definitive marital consummation, the relationship would float on forever. What is particularly puzzling about the current male reluctance to take on the responsibilities of marriage as compared to their fathers and grandfathers who entered matrimony with equanimity is the minimized risk of today's groom. Gone is the old head-of-the-household financial burden borne solely by the man; gone is the "till death do us part" burden that meant a life sentence. Today, the majority of women work and share the financial onus with their husbands, and divorce is as American as apple pie.

Tom's decision to marry Ellen finally came about under pressure of the old squeeze play tactic wherein he is given the option of making the commitment or losing the lady. Ellen made it plain that although she loved him, she was seeking a future of marriage and family, and if he did not see himself as a willing partner in this plan, she could no longer waste her valuable time.

As usual, once the wedding plans got under way, Tom was swept up in the euphoria of his new status: fiancé. Good wishes, gifts, celebrations welcoming them to both families—all of this swirled around them happily creating the new reality of Ellen and Tom as A Couple. Acceptance and approval were palpable, reinforcing their belief that they were doing The Right Thing.

Of course, like all imminent brides and grooms, they experienced moments of doubt. "He's intellectual and enjoys ballet and opera and theatre, but why won't he talk about it after the performance? It's so stimulating to discuss what we've just seen. How could I live with a person who hates to deal with the abstract and doesn't enjoy mental gymnastics?" "I love her and admire how fast her mind works, but it's tiring doing all that analyzing and dissecting of emotions that she demands after we see a play. Is she going to be a pain in the head all my life?"

They argued a bit, discussed their differences and worried about them privately but not too seriously. They were both deeply in love, and there was the fun of working out a life together . . . finding an apartment, selecting furniture. Events moved along and soon they were married with ceremony, celebration and ritual that underscored to both of them the true solemnity and seriousness of the commitment they had made.

The first few months of marriage were exciting because they were developing a new life. It was a time of discoveries, some bringing delight and some dread. Ellen was charmed to learn that Tom enjoyed cooking weekend breakfasts. He had evolved a method of coddling eggs that delivered creamy whites and yolks, a point of which he was especially proud, and he loved the procedure of cooking and presenting Ellen with beautifully served breakfasts. Precise and neat, Tom worked systematically and left the kitchen immaculate. The downside was that he expected the same culinary organization from her. Ellen was what she called an "impulsive cook" which meant that counters were covered with ingredients and utensils that she might decide to use in whatever dish was under way, and Ellen's kitchen-in-work looked like, as Tom put it, she was preparing dinner for a Serbian regiment.

There were other annoyances involving habits. Tom complained about Ellen's need to hang her just-worn clothing on bedroom closet doors "to air out." "What for? You shower daily, you use deodorants. Why do you think your clothes smell . . . from what?" and he muttered nightly about the difficulties of trying to fall asleep in the midst of a rummage sale. For the most part, he complained about her habits and she complained about his complaining about her habits. "Prussian!" she called him. "Gypsy!" he called her. She worried about being hounded for life by a nitpicking nudnik and he worried about spending his life with a slob.

But these were minor skirmishes. The major area of emotional conflict was Tom's career. Ellen's business life was structured, directed and satisfying; Tom's was amorphous anarchy. His days were spent waiting for calls from his agent with assignments for magazine articles, or from advertising agency creative directors offering free-lance copywriting jobs.

He was paid well for his work because he was talented, and when the jobs and checks came in he regarded the world as a wondrous playground and was a delight to live with. But the fallow periods were torture to both of them. Filled with fears about his ability and future, Tom would mope around the house during the day and be a total bust in bed at night. The corrosive despair destroyed his sex drive as one failure fed upon the other; inability to function during the day led to inability to function at night and self-doubts about his talent were further compounded by doubts about his manhood.

Inevitably it would all culminate in one night's bursting forth of expressions of doubt and desolation as he lay in bed next to Ellen, both unable to sleep because of his anguish. Ellen loved Tom and she suffered to see him suffer. Also she was brought up as are all women to be supportive, sympathetic and sustaining to men. So she would launch into a talk of reassurance, to build belief in himself, and to give him direction and confidence. Smart and perceptive, she listened to his tales of failures—jobs he did not get, assignments that were cancelled—and then give him keen analyses of the reasons for the disappointments followed by recommendations of how to prevent recurrences. Tom had tremendous respect for Ellen's judgment and he listened carefully, his spirits lifting as she outlined a program of potential success. Then always he would look at her lovingly and say, "You're so wonderful, so smart. What have I done to deserve you? You should have married a dentist and had an easy life," followed by an affectionate kiss, a deep sigh of contentment and then, totally relaxed, off to sleep in seconds. But where did this leave Ellen? Although she spoke to Tom with great certainty about his inevitable success, she had her nagging doubts. Did he have the right stuff to make it? How could she really know? After all, the world was filled with talented writers, how could one be sure that Tom would succeed at this competitive craft?

"Do I want to spend my life with a man who might never make a living? I love his admiring and needing me, but do I want to face a future with someone who will constantly draw upon my strength for emotional support?"

But as time went on, these nocturnal guidance counselling sessions became less frequent as Tom's work flow improved due to Ellen's suggestions and the growing self-confidence he projected. Concurrently, Tom's love for Ellen grew, as did his joy in the married state. As a result, his carping on her personal habits turned into affectionate tolerance, even converted into causes for commendation. "My wife is immaculate about her clothing. She won't put anything into her closet until it's been aired thoroughly." "Ellen is such a creative cook. She just gets an idea and goes wherever it takes her and it's always great." Of course, Ellen blossomed under Tom's burgeoning belief in her, in them, and his obvious pride and love. Her friends began to tell her enviously that she was a lucky woman to have found such a great guy and have such a happy marriage. And she agreed.

Do You Know Me?
Do I Know Me?

The old saw that "you never know someone until you live with him" may be true. But so what? The real heart of adjusting to marriage is to become aware that you never really know *yourself* until you live with someone. What sort of emotions does your partner's behavior evoke in you? Do you like the person he/she makes you into? Do you like the YOU you become from living with this person?

Ellen entered marriage with the subconscious belief that Tom was not the sort of man she should have married. She had been societally brainwashed to believe that being a "strong woman" is undesirable, and that she needed a "powerful man" to relegate her to the acceptably subordinate position. Inge Broverman's mid-sixties studies on the desirable traits of mentally healthy people asked therapists to define "healthy male" and "healthy female." The majority of the therapists indicated that a "healthy male" was "active, independent, competitive and logical." Whereas the "healthy female" was "dependent, subjective, passive and illogical."

So here we have Ellen uncertain about her role in the marriage and the aptness of her being "the strong one." And we have Tom seeing his wife go off to her important job each day while he is never sure where, if ever, his next assignment is coming from. Did she feel used? Did he feel undervalued? It could have happened that way, with these feelings festering and ultimately forcing the end of the marriage. But it didn't because each one discovered reactive emotions to the other's behavior that made them feel happier with themselves.

Tom's burden in life had always been the insecurity that men who will never make a million feel about their self-worth. Charming, handsome, intelligent, he had all the attributes for personal success but none for financial success, and since that's how men are measured, Tom felt unsettled and unsure.

Ellen's strength gave him the rock he needed. The feeling that with her at his side, he had to make it, made his self-assurance grow. He loved Ellen more and more because she made him into the Tom he liked, and always wanted to be.

Ellen, bred to be fearful of being the dominant one in a relationship, discovered she liked being free to be herself and use her brain and ability without danger of retaliation from an angered, diminished male. She enjoyed the adoration and admiration her intelligent guidance evoked from Tom. She felt important, she felt loved, she felt feminine. She liked the Ellen person she now was, and loved Tom because he made her so.

The Caretaking Need

In the interviews I conducted for this book, one question elicited a startling similarity of answers. "What did you want from marriage?" The answer I heard in almost 90 percent of those interviewed was, "To be taken care of." The interesting thing was that although the wording of the answers was similar, the meanings were diverse. When pressed further, one 49-year-old male production manager said, "I need emotional support, someone to cheer me up when I'm down." A number of women in their thirties and forties explained it as having someone to take care of getting the car fixed, repairs around the house, and managing the monies. Many men (aged late forties and over) stated simply, "I want a wife to take care of me when I get sick," a frequent concern of those becoming aware of their own mortality.

As you can see, many of these definitions came

from hindsight. Recognition of true inner needs requires a depth of self-understanding that few people have; most of us become aware of needs only when the fulfillment stops. The production manager's wife had become very ill and could no longer provide the conjugal confabs that gave him the emotional support he had taken for granted during all the years of their happy marriage. A few of the women had suddenly been thrown totally on their own for periods while husbands recuperated from major illnesses.

To be taken care of is a very basic need, but only works well when there is symbiosis. A child needs to be taken care of; the mother enjoys the fulfillment of nurturing. The marital relationship is taking care of one another's needs. But how can you tell in advance what those needs truly are? You can't; you must give yourself a chance to live through it and allow your true needs to emerge. Marriage is the building of a small personal world in which matters of joint physical, fiscal and emotional comfort are handled by each partner in the consigned role. It doesn't matter who does what as long as both husband and wife are happy with the roles and the results. "Marriage is that relation between man and woman in which the independence is equal, the dependence mutual and the obligation mutual," said Louis Kaufman Anspacher.

The risk at the Entry Level is that the partners do not give themselves the chance to find out what parts they really wish to take in the construction of their life together. There is no preparation for this decision-making process, only the process itself.

* * *

Nan and Elliot were a golden couple. They had all the surface successes that inspired envy or disgust, depending on your social values. They lived in a stunningly decorated co-op apartment in the most fashionable section of the city, had impeccable parties at which all the up-to-the-minute food specialties were served, and travelled extensively and expensively. They were married two years ago after a stormy on-again-off-again courtship of a year. Nan was 35, a highly successful jewelry designer. Elliot was an investment banker who, at 40, had just ended a disastrous marriage. Nan had never been married and the concept of total dependency on one man frightened her. She saw herself as an independent person who had made a place in a highly competitive field and she was reluctant to relinquish any of her hard-won individuality. But she had fallen madly in love with Elliot and wanted very much to spend her life with him. Loath to burn her bridges behind her, rather than give up her lovely small apartment she subleased it for two years. She was stepping into marriage while keeping an eye on the exits.

The first problem arose when Elliot handed her money "for the household," as he had been accustomed to do with his previous wife.

"What the hell is this?" she asked. "I make my own money—I don't need handouts from you."

As Nan saw it, this move was a threat to her independence—didn't men always try to control women with money? Wasn't this just the way of establishing dominant-subordinate roles? Elliot was dumbfounded. He told Nan that he was thoroughly delighted with her career success, and it was a source of great pride to him to have an achieving wife. He told her that in no way did he wish to change her into a submissive female living a derivative existence. She told him she was glad of that because in no way would she permit it. They talked it over, and evolved a method of handling their joint finances that was satisfactory to them both. There were flare-ups from time to time involving role definitions. She: "Pick up your own damned shirts. That's not my job." He: "Why don't you take out the garbage? Where is it written that it's my job?"

But once Nan felt comfortable in the new role of "Mrs." without concern that her individuality was being compromised, and Elliot understood her need to assert this position, their lives settled down into a pleasant connubial routine. Suddenly provided with a spacious luxuriously equipped kitchen, Nan began to experiment with cooking and found she loved every aspect of planning the menu, buying the ingredients and preparing the food. Cookbooks began to supplant the sociological treatises that used to be stacked up on her nighttable. And Elliot, ever the sybarite, enjoyed the marvelous meals that awaited him every night. But if you serve superb food, the accoutrements must be suitable. So Nan began haunting the antique shops and department stores to pick up unusual serving pieces and napery. She found that she became annoyed when professional demands on her time interfered with her new interests, and she began to turn down design commissions.

Since Elliot's business required a great deal of entertaining of clients, Nan suggested he invite them to dinner at home rather than the former routine of taking them to restaurants, "It's so much more personal," she said. Elliot began to bring guests to Nan's perfectly cooked and elegantly served dinners, and was wondrously proud of her accomplishments. The kitchen and dining room were the focal points of Nan's new interests, but inevitably she branched out into the surrounding rooms. The bedroom needed redoing, which meant a three-month-search for just the right provincial wallpaper to complement the antique armoire she found at one of the auction sales she began to frequent.

Within two years after they were married, Nan had dropped out of the jewelry design field except for once-in-a-while calls from some of her old customers, and was revelling in the role of homemaker. And Elliot who had never experienced such total care of his needs was deliriously happy.

Here was a couple who had entered the marriage with firmly fixed ideas of what they wanted, needed and expected from the arrangement. Nan had a self-image of the dynamic career woman, and Elliot saw himself as the archetypical modern male who would have a successful wife. But take away the pressures of the feminist movement, and you have two people who want to live the way their parents did with husband bringing home the bacon and wife cooking it. She liked to nurture and he liked being nurtured. But given the current mores, how could any modern couple admit to such heresy?

As in most successful marital adjustments, there was no sudden epiphany. "My God, I really want to stay home—I really hate working." It happened freely. According to Dr. Roger L. Gould: "Whether she chooses a career in or out of the home, a woman who chooses freely will worry less about making the 'right' choice. A woman who stops herself from making the career choice she really wants because of a childhood consciousness fear of the results of taking that other road must live with the tension caused by her denial."*

Very wisely, Nan and Elliot never went through the highly overrated process of "talking it out." What would have been gained by admitting they had been totally wrong in their pre-conceived portraits of themselves and their needs? Of course, if these shifting roles were not satisfactory to them both . . . if Nan loved her new life but Elliot was disappointed in and ashamed of his wife who opted for the traditional homemaker role, then certainly discussions would be necessary. But it happened easily, and they just moved along naturally and happily into a new level of marriage.

Alike vs. Unlike

Whether opposites attract or repel has been a matter of debate forever. Aristotle said, "Many lovers . . . are constant, if familiarity has led them to love each other's characters, these being alike." Heraclitus said, "From different tones come the fairest tune." Every unmarried person has a preconception of what he or she wants and needs in a mate, usually based on omnibus opinions drilled into him/her during their lifetimes. Parents and family will categorize a child early on because it makes life simpler; it's easier to deal with people once you've pigeon-holed them. "She's outgoing, he's introverted; she's stubborn, he's headstrong; he's a dreamer, she's practical and sensible" and so on—these labels once applied tend to stick forever. And so, burdened with these prepackaged personality

**Transformations: Growth and Change in Adult Life,* New York: Simon and Schuster, 1978, p. 57.

analyses, the grownup children go out in the world seeking mates with complementing qualities. "I am weak, I need strength." "I'm shy, I need an extrovert."

But successful marriages are not based on complemental qualities, but on complemental *needs*. The whole adult is a composite of his/her experiences, reactions, likes, dislikes, loves and hates. These exposures to life, added to an individual's innate makeup, create *needs*. And what a person needs to live happily may be a total surprise to himself as well as his friends and family.

* * *

One of the best marriages I encountered was between Bill, a quiet, cultured man, and Alice, a woman whose main interest was shopping and who accompanied him to the opera only so that she could have reason to display her latest dress. Before they married, Bill's best friend felt it his duty to warn Bill of the certain misery of spending life with a woman with whom a serious conversation was out of the question.

"After you've seen a great movie, read a marvelous book, who can you discuss it with?" Bill smiled and answered, "You," and then went on to say that he did not need this function from a wife.

Bill had spent the previous year living with a woman who was a psychiatric social worker, and she, as Bill put it, "analyzed our relationship to death. I've had all the probing discussions I'll need for a lifetime."

What Bill loved about Alice was her simple common sense, her intuitive handling of his need for privacy and separateness, and her total acceptance of him as he was. According to *Husbands and Wives:*

A Nationwide Study of Marriage, by Anthony Pietropinto and Jacqueline Simenauer,* "Some successful couples maintain the illusion of 'sharing everything,' but a more realistic successful approach seems to be admitting that large portions of one another's existence will forever lie outside the direct experience of the spouse without adversely affecting the hours and experiences that can be truly shared."

On a simplistic label-to-label basis for coupling, it should have been a disaster. He is an introvert. She is placid and cannot "draw him out" as the marriage maivins require. He's an intellectual, her idea of entertainment is a Broadway musical and a Harold Robbins novel. But she has a different kind of intelligence than Bill's, a practical mind and an intuitive sense of how to handle people and make them happy. Bill admires and respects those abilities, just as she admires and respects his. Their personalities might not dovetail, but their needs do.

Three Lives Are Better Than One

One of the main causes of unnecessary stress during the Entry Level is the struggle trying to work out how two people can live one life. But that's wrong. Because marriage is the establishment of *three* lives—his, hers and theirs—and the meshing of these three units into a single harmonious entity is the real goal.

If they are a working couple, he has his working life, she has hers, and the balance of their time is spent on their third life—the marriage. They may

*New York: Times Books, 1979, p. 133.

bring some of their work lives home, they may not, but whatever the arrangement, both husband and wife must regard it as equitable or there can be trouble.

* * *

Mara is the marketing manager of a computer company. Her husband of three months, Anthony, is an assistant professor of Anthropology at a major midwestern university. At the end of a busy day at the office, Mara looked forward to coming home and regaling Anthony with details of the crises and confrontations she had worked her way through. She loved her job and regarded everything about it with enthusiasm and tremendous concern. So much so that she failed to notice that Anthony never asked what kind of a day she had, and found reasons to constantly leave the room during her litanies about the problems and successes of the day. When she finally ran out of steam and subjects, he would sit down with his pre-prandial cocktail and tell her in exhaustive detail about all the politics of academia that were driving him up the wall and about the performances of some of his more interesting students. Until one evening when Mara was discussing an issue of tremendous importance to her—the marketing of a new product that was to be her sole responsibility—and Anthony dozed off. She looked at his closed eyes and sagging body with incredulity and then exploded.

"You're not interested in what I do, yet you expect me to listen to all that academic chickenshit you spout every night!" And the battle was joined. After much screaming and back-and-forth accusations of selfishness, lack of caring, the real truth emerged.

Said Anthony: "Who really gives a flying fuck about how many pieces of software get sold to some money-grubbing businessmen so they produce more junk and make even more money?"

Mara stopped dead as she realized the full import of his statement.

"You mean you think that my work is less important than yours—and that what I do isn't worth talking about?"

Shamefacedly he admitted that maybe there was a kernel of truth here. Mara looked at him and said in cold fury:

"And you think your stories about how John Gellman is boinking the chairwoman of his department so that she'll back him when he comes up for tenure review indicate what great contributions to society you people in academia are making? You're a bunch of crass money-grubbers just like the rest of us and you're all out to save your asses and not the world. The only difference between you and us is we're honest about admitting why we do what we do!"

From that point on, the discussion turned to constructive issues. Anthony admitted to Mara and to himself that maybe his feelings were somewhat based on jealously because Mara made more money than he did, and demeaning her work helped him to elevate his own self-esteem. And perhaps he was a little concerned that her enthusiasm for work was greater than her interest in him. Then both admitted to being just a bit jealous of each other's other life and their involvements in people and activities outside of the marriage. Once that was out in the open, they were able to work it out. Each admitted to not being sufficiently aware of the other's needs and reactions, and vowed to change. Both felt the need to share their professional lives with the other and so agreed to continue their policy of discussing the details of their work. But now it would be with sensitivity, and the comfort of knowing that their outside pursuits in no way impinged upon the importance and solidity of the marriage.

What worked for Mara and Anthony might not be the solution for other couples. Many people do not like to bring their work home. "Who wants to talk about my work hassles at night?" said one factory foreman. "My wife tells me I'm not sharing my life with her, but to me it would just be living through the aggravations all over again." When he explained how he felt and his wife realized that she was not being consciously shut out because he didn't value her input, the constant "Why don't you talk to me?" battles ceased.

The main point here is that marriage must be the merging of three lives. You may look upon your profession as merely a means of making money so you can enjoy your non-working hours. Or you may regard your career as an integral part of your being and the vital element that defines you. Or a mixture of the above. But your work day is separate from that of your spouse, and that's your other life. You may choose to bring it into your married life, or not, as long as you both agree on the degree. One woman I interviewed told me that she loved hearing about her husband's work because it was so interesting, but she had no desire for equal time because, as she put it, "At the end of the day, I've had it." Another woman I spoke to complained that her husband wanted to talk about her work because he felt he could make a real contribution. "He really knows nothing about my job and his suggestions are usually a pain in the neck and all wrong.

So we finally cut out any work talk and things are smoother."

He's happy, she's happy, they're happy. That's all that matters.

My Friends and Family & Your Friends and Family

Barbara is in a snit again because Scott lunched yesterday with an old girlfriend.

"But she's just a friend—there's nothing romantic here," he proclaimed for the fourteenth time. "She's always been just a friend. Are you telling me that because I'm married I can't see my old friends?"

But Barbara refused to accept that Scott had no sexual interest in his female friend. "If you love me, why do you want to see her?" And she made it into a contest.

This fight had been going on during the entire four months of their marriage. Although every other aspect of their relationship was good, this area was a major source of difficulty. Scott, aged 32, was a gregarious man who had accumulated many friends in his lifetime, both male and female, and he had held on to every one he had ever known since sixth grade. Barbara, on the other hand, was a shy, solitary type who clung to togetherness with Scott and felt that he and she must share all social occasions. Although she understood his friendship with men friends, she was hurt when he spent an evening with "the guys." And she looked with great suspicion upon any meetings with women friends.

Scott tried to explain, he pleaded, he assured Barbara that his need for and pleasure in spending time with friends of both sexes in no way affected the great love he had for her. She listened, she tried to understand, and from time to time would profess to accept and appreciate his position. But every time Scott mentioned his lunch with a woman friend, a shadow passed over Barbara's face and she turned silent.

"It's no use," she said. "I try to believe what you tell me, but I can't stop hurting every time I hear you've seen another woman. It's unreasonable, irrational. I understand that because I feel that way doesn't mean you have to. But I cannot control my reaction."

Seeing his old friends was very important to Scott, and he was angered by Barbara's restrictions. But he loved her deeply, and enjoyed their life together. And soon, where before he would call one of his woman friends whenever the whim hit him, he now found himself hesitating before calling, and often as not killed the impulse. The argument with Barbara was just not worth it. Seeing someone was weighed on a value scale: is this meeting worth the pain it will cause Barbara, and the inevitable argument that will result? As so, in time, Scott stopped seeing his women friends alone and compromised by having them over for dinner with both him and his wife.

Scott could have pushed, insisted, and fought on. Sure it was not fair that because of Barbara's insecurity he was deprived of the pleasures of his old relationships. But where is it written that life is fair? As the character on a TV sitcom told her daughter who protested that her mother's interdiction against dating was not fair, "Fair? Fair is where cowboys throw buffalo chips at each other. Life is not fair."

Marriage, like life, is a series of compromises,

both conscious and subconscious. Everything is a trade-off, and if you resist that rule, you'll never make it to the Second Level of marriage. Or life. Scott could have continued to see his women friends and lie to Barbara about it. That was another choice. But since marriage must have trust to survive, such dissembling would inevitably erode the relationship. Scott made his choice, albeit subconsciously and gradually. As in any developing relationship, it is a matter of reacting to reactions. He dreaded dealing with Barbara's response to his behavior, so found himself hesitating to take the steps that would cause friction between them. And gradually he adjusted his behavior. It was unjust, perhaps, but for him it was not worth breaking up a marriage over.

Similar Entry Level disputes ensue over familial obligations. The most major recurring fight my husband and I had during the early years of marriage was over my insistence on visiting my brother. No matter how I would emphasize the importance of maintaining family ties, that I loved my brother and wanted to keep a relationship with him, my husband would balk. We tried to analyze his reluctance, and decided that he was envious of my brother's having the paternal support both financial and emotional that my husband had never enjoyed, his parents having divorced when he was ten years old. That did not help one bit; knowledge does not always create solutions. Even in later years when my husband's financial success outstripped my brother's, the distaste for visiting persisted. Twenty years later we finally both realized the real reason for the problem: my husband hated to see the "me" I became on these visits. Both of them smug and judgmental (my husband referred to impending visits to their home as going to Mt. Olympus), my brother and sister-in-law's criticism and condescension toward things we thought and did caused me to put on a frenetic bonhomie to allay my apprehension.

But look, you must expect that there will always be some things you will fight over without destroying the fiber of your marriage. The trick during the Entry Level years is to maintain your sense of proportion on the importance of the issues at issue. "At the beginning there was the Word." And at the end is "the last word." What satisfaction will you derive from having the last word if it leads to the end of your marriage? It is amazing how unimportant some seemingly vital points can become to you in time. Give yourself a chance to find out.

Sexual Adjustment: Are You Kidding?

If you think that sexual adjustments have to be made during the early days of marriage, where have you been living? Gone are the days where the mother-in-law proudly hung out the blood-stained sheet on the morning after the nuptials to proclaim the proven virginity of her daughter-in-law. Unless they have a religious taboo against pre-marital intercourse, there are few couples who enter marriage today without having slept together, let alone lived together.

However, if they have had sex but not lived together, there could be some adjustments as to frequency and consistency of performance. They will have to live with each other's "headaches"—the times when weariness, upset or plain disinterest of the moment brings about turndowns—and not regard every "no" to sex as a personal rejection.

Sexual problems will crop up during the subsequent levels of marriage as new elements enter the marital relationship. But we'll come to that later.

You've Passed the Entry Level: How Do You Know?

No bells go off, and no one hands you a diploma upon completion of this first phase of your marriage. The way you will know that you have indeed become A Married Couple is when you notice that during and after an argument, all you feel is anger. You no longer put the fight on The Scorecard on which you have been subconsciously rating your marriage and weighing its viability.

In other words, you no longer think to yourself:

"If this bitch/bastard keeps giving me this kind of trouble, I'll just take off."

Every day is no longer Judgment Day. You accept each other, warts and all. It's no longer him and me or her and me—it's Us.

It's time to feel a great satisfaction in what you both have accomplished. The Entry Level is the biggest hurdle of all because it is the period of the greatest number of adjustments. Remember that you came into a new world carrying the burdensome baggage of preconceptions and expectations—some realistic, some fantastic—plus the frightening thought that unlike all other life-altering directions you have taken (new schools, new jobs, new homes) this is the first one that is to be *forever*. The word in itself is off-putting, but the only way to avoid thinking in awesomely cosmic terms is to take it day by day and not to endow every statement, every action and reaction as a portent of the future.

To regard any behavior as eternal at this stage of marriage is ridiculous. At this point, the only constant is that things will change. According to Carl Jung, "The meeting of two personalities is like the contact of two chemical substances: if there is any reaction, both are transformed."*

If he, for instance, doesn't show as much affection as you would like—a common complaint about husbands who tend to have difficulty being demonstrative since it used to be regarded as feminine and weak—give him a chance to learn how important kissing, caressing and small attentions are to you. He will change if he loves you because he will want to make you happy. If she is inconsiderate of your need for solitude and separateness, give her a chance to learn that it is not a rejection but merely an important personal requirement of yours that in no way affects your life together. In fact, it will enhance and help nurture the growth of your marriage. As defined by Rilke, "A good marriage is that in which each appoints the other guardian of his solitude. . . . Once the realization is accepted that even between the *closest* human beings infinite distances continue to exist, a wonderful living side by side can grow up, if they succeed in loving the distance between them which makes it possible for each to see the other whole against the sky."**

The Entry Level is a period of discovery, pleasure and pain. You will learn things about yourself that will surprise you, one of them undoubtedly being that you have a much higher level of tolerance than you dreamed. I have seen people accept character traits and behavior in spouses that would have

**Modern Man in Search of a Soul*, New York: Harcourt, 1939.

***The Letters of Rainer Maria Rilke*, New York: Norton, 1969.

caused the instant death of any friendship. Because, putting it quite simply, the payoff is greater. The pleasures of living with and sharing experiences with someone you love and enjoy is impossible to appreciate and describe until you live it. Quoting Jung once more: "Seldom, or perhaps never, does marriage develop into an individual relationship smoothly and without crises: there is no coming to consciousness without pain."* It takes time, it takes effort, it takes sensitivity, it takes growth—but it's worth it.

**Contributions to Analytical Psychology*, 1928.

THE SECOND LEVEL

Acceptance

(The Good Times Begin)

It's "Us" Now!

This is for keeps. You feel married, you're comfortable with the words "my husband," "my wife". You may even be able to call your in-laws "Mom" and "Dad" instead of waiting for them to turn around before you begin a conversation.

The scoreboard has disappeared, and slights, annoyances and transgressions are handled with overt reactions instead of being entered subconsciously, or consciously, on the grievance list. And your reactions will probably be the opposite of your Entry Level responses: Where before you might have blown your stack when you found her nylons soaking in the sink, now you put them on the side of the basin and go about your business without a word, or maybe even rinse them out! When you find he left the empty soda bottle and box of crackers on the table, you no longer put things away in sullen anger, hugging your resentment to yourself, but let it all out with "Who do you think will put your stuff away . . . the good tooth fairy?"

You feel free . . . free to release your resentments,

free to make demands. "How about you making dinner for a change? You cooked before we were married. . . . It's just like riding a bicycle, you never lose the touch."

You are accepted and accepting and are not worried about making waves or endangering the relationship.

At this point let me repeat the statement made by the woman who had been married for fifty years who, when asked the secret of the longevity of the relationship, answered: "Overlooking. . . . I overlooked a lot, he overlooked a lot—we got along."

What you find in the Acceptance stage of marriage is that you are overlooking minor annoyances, perhaps even major ones. Why? Because you have realized either consciously or subconsciously that disagreement isn't death to a marriage and your scoreboard has shown you that you can live with differences. In fact, the happiness of some couples depends on dispute; it keeps the juices flowing.

One couple who obviously adored each other and had been married for thirty years were an embarrassment to be with because of the abuse they heaped on each other publicly. "Louise, you don't know what the hell you're talking about," he would interrupt in the middle of an impassioned statement she was making about the state of the economy. Since she was a highly successful business executive, her opinions were based on facts and not conjecture and his interruption replete with epithets such as "ignoramus" and "jerk" invariably got them started on a round of insults that were horrifying to the listeners. Most of us felt that if our spouses had performed in that mortifying manner we would have sunk into the upholstery, and not spoken to them for a week. But these two were obviously delighted with each other and positively relished the battle, totally unconcerned about their audience. In fact, many people in the room seemed equally unconcerned. Those turned out to be the denigrating duo's oldest friends who were obviously accustomed to these flareups. These friends knew that, catastrophic as they seemed, these major confrontations would have no effect upon the couple's very happy relationship. If anything, dispute stimulated it.

A man I interviewed who had been divorced many years ago and was looking desperately to remarry told me how he had just broken up with a woman whom he was missing terribly. I asked the natural question "Then why did you break up with her?" "Because her negatives outweighed her positives and I felt we could never make it together." I immediately understood why he had not remarried and probably never would. There is absolutely no way you can tell in advance what constitutes an insurmountable negative until you have lived with it and all the lovely positives. You do not know how much you are willing to give up until you learn how much you enjoy what you get in return. This man told me how much he loved the warmth and affection his ex-womanfriend displayed, the touching and hugging and kissing. And how he had never realized how important these traits were to him. If he had been willing to take the risk of tossing out the scoreboard and stopped balancing qualifications like a checkbook, he might have found that the pleasures of living day-to-day with a person who made him feel loved and nurtured relegated many of the "negatives" into relative unimportance.

The "Acceptance Level" begins the best part of marriage, the wonderful sense of "us." You both automatically consider situations from a joint viewpoint—what *we* want to do. A good gauge of how far into acceptance you are is when you find yourself instantly rejecting an invitation because you instinctively know that your spouse would find it unpleasant. Your partner's likes and dislikes become built-in to your decision-making mechanism. You don't resent the limitations imposed, you don't even think about them. Often as not this new joint perspective expands your activities rather than reduces them. You do things your spouse enjoys for the pure pleasure of sharing his or her enjoyment. One of the greatest joys of the marital relationship is the enhancement of shared experiences. You learn from one another and absorb each other's tastes until a new sense of joint appreciation emerges.

The build-up of these shared experiences becomes the solid basis of your marriage. The mutual recollections of your past together become the bedrock of your future. Sometimes it was happiness, other times it was misery, but a tremendous bond was forged when you underwent it together.

Another sign of acceptance is the quiet understanding of each other that enables you to act intuitively without the need to "communicate" your feelings about every minor issue.

Communication—The Marriage Killer

Every marriage manual, every self-help book on marriage stresses the vital need of "communication" between husband and wife. Don't seethe, don't build resentments—speak up, let each other know what's bugging you. But those books were written before the current era of the "communication explosion." Nobody keeps anything to themselves any more, it's simply not fashionable. In the old days when you asked someone, "How are you?" you expected an answer concerning the state of his health. Today you get the condition of his or her psyche in full, painfully personal and usually boring detail. Everybody is an armchair psychiatrist, and introspection and psyche-searching and talking about it are the style.

In a marriage this can be death. You are together a great deal . . . days, hours, months, years. If you develop the habit of evaluating your emotional reaction to every move the other person makes, and if you indulge yourself in the habit of discussing each other's annoying traits, you'll drive each other crazy and create a wedge that could become immovable. This is a case of "less is more." What starts out as "communication" becomes confrontation, and relationships cannot survive too many of those. I am not suggesting that you act like the couple in the Dorothy Parker story whose divorce shocked their friends because they seemed like such a happy couple who never fought. What actually happened was their lack of conversation resulted in boring each other to death. But the current tendency to tell each other how you feel about everything puts a heavy burden on a marriage.

Of course, certain things your mate does will be irksome. Before you register your complaint, evaluate the importance of the issue—to your spouse and to you. Is this behavior pattern or habit something that is really important to him/her? And how seriously are you hurt by it? If it is something that wounds you deeply and continuation will have a corrosive effect on your relationship, then by all means discuss it. But if it is just annoying, creating borderline bother, don't mention it . . . let it go. Some people come to a marriage with the idea that they must strip the spouse down and expose every aspect of the heart, soul and psyche in order to achieve full intimacy. But must you know exactly how a machine works before you enjoy working with it?

When You Know It's Forever

One of the questions I asked everyone interviewed for this book was: "What was the point in your marriage when you knew it was 'for good'—that you had passed into the Acceptance Level?" One of the most powerful examples of how a single occurrence created the epiphany of realization that the union would be forever was told to me by a man who was now in the fourteenth year of a happy marriage.

"Ann and I got married young; we were in love, wanted to be together, and that seemed the right step to take. We were both working and going to school at night, so we had very little time to really work things out between us. We were both so exhausted that fighting took too much energy. Then she became pregnant, totally unexpectedly. We had a daughter and then another. She was home with two babies, I was busting my ass to try to build a business, she resented my absences, I resented her resentments. Oh, we had some slambang battles, but we loved each other and just sort of kept on going because neither one really wanted 'out' although there were plenty of times when I thought of it, and I know my wife did too. We had decided that two children was our limit and our family was complete. Then she became pregnant. It was an accident, sloppiness, call it what you want, but to us it was a disaster. We talked about abortion, neither of us has any moral or religious objection to a woman choosing to have an abortion. We agonized over it and decided to go ahead with the birth. Neither of us could face the concept of doing away with our child. And then Ann got the measles, a severe case and in her third month. The doctor told us that there was an 80 percent chance that the child would be born deformed or defective and we should consider abortion. If you think we agonized before, that was amateur night. We decided together that we would go through with it. We prayed for six months. And I went through the natural childbirth course with Ann although we had not done this with our other children, but this birth we felt had to be undergone as much as possible by both of us together. When we saw that beautiful, healthy baby boy come out, Ann and I looked at each other and without a word exchanged we both knew this marriage was forever."

As he told me this story, his eyes filled and he was silent for a moment. "What happened to us was that we shared an event that was so important, it changed both of us. We had a sense of having lived through a major life crisis that involved only us in the whole world, and now together we were invincible."

Most of the time, the awareness of having passed over a threshhold is not so definitive. It's not like you wake up one day and say, "We've made it; our marriage is established and for good." It happens gradually, in an imperceptible evolutionary fashion. You suddenly find that you are no longer thinking just of what I want and he/she wants, but what *we* want, and you talk of future plans for years ahead. It is an admission that you have decided to spend your lives together. The tentative quality of the relationship disappears and is replaced by an implicit sense of permanence. If you take the time to stop and listen, you may hear the wonderfully companionable sounds of silence. Fights are fewer because each has come to accede a bit to the other's demands. The defensiveness that made you battle for your right to maintain your individuality evaporates as you realize that you have not been diminished but, rather, have merged into a new entity called Us. This new joint unit is so satisfying that you wonder why you didn't get to it years ago.

The Termination of Territories

"You tend to back away from issues that you know he's touchy about," said a Missouri woman who had been married for five years. "You just think, 'It's really not important enough to make a big thing over.' And you let things slide that years ago you would have screamed your head off about. I just stopped hassling him about helping me around the house even though we both work. It used to burn me up how we'd come home at night and I'd head for the kitchen and he'd grab a Scotch and go for the TV. One day I had to work late and when I got home, he'd made dinner and sort of tidied up the place. I tell you I was flabbergasted. I didn't say anything and things just sort of changed and he started filling in and doing things around the place that he'd never touch before."

Finish the Fight Over Finances

Now it's time to settle down to the details of assigning duties, and since you're past the jockeying for position stage, you're free to give the job to the best qualified applicant. At least, that's the ideal, but frequently egos and misapprehensions get in the way.

* * *

Chuck was a mathematician and computer whiz. So of course he decided he should handle the finances and the checkbook. Karen had been brought up, as have most women, to think that she was totally inept with figures and calculations, so she gladly turned the details of the management of their finances over to her husband.

During the first few years of their marriage, their monies were in a muddle.

There was the time Karen was mortified in a store when they told her they could not accept her credit card since it was overextended. Once the electricity was turned off because Chuck forgot to pay the bill. She got used to dunning calls from various creditors. And then there was the terrible ordeal of the one evening each month that Chuck worked to reconcile their checkbook and pay bills. Karen just hid herself in the other room with a book so she couldn't hear the fury and imprecations that Chuck hurled at the bank, the government and the world at large as he struggled to make the numbers match. There were also shreiking accusations leveled at her for not entering a check legibly. Or battles over the need for some of her expenditures. It was an evening Karen dreaded but accepted as inevitable.

During the early days of their marriage, she had suggested to Chuck that maybe she could try to take over the job, since she did have a brain and a calculator, and as far as she could see that's all that was needed.

"You handle the money? Are you kidding? I'm a mathematician; what do you know about figures? You'd bankrupt us in a month."

The male ego at work.

They had been married for two years, and it was Chuck's night to do the books, but he had come home with a miserable migraine. The stuff was all laid out on the table, when suddenly he turned to Karen, who was walking into the kitchen, and said:

"I'm beat. How about you taking a stab at this?"

Karen was flabbergasted. She sent Chuck off to bed with an ice pack, and then sat down to face the challenge. Within one hour she had completed paying all the bills and reconciling the checkbook. She was delighted with herself. She walked into the darkened bedroom and said, "How are you feeling, honey? You don't have to worry about the bills and checks, it's all done."

Chuck sighed in relief. "Great. I hate that stinkin' job. It's yours."

What happened here, as with the Missouri man who was now willing to get involved with household chores, was the cessation of hostilities in the Battle for Territories that occurs during the Entry Level period. Each partner has been fighting to establish claims to what was envisioned as his territory, her territory, his job, her job. Fearful that any sign of willingness to yield his position as macho master of the home could compromise his ownership of that vital territory in the marriage, one husband refused to perform any household task, and the other refused to relinquish his role as the financial manager. It is probable that in these men's childhood homes their fathers performed specific jobs which the sons regarded as symbolic male responsibilities. But once the vying for position in the marriage was over and they settled into the Acceptance Level, it became "our home," "our dinner," "our checkbook," and who did what mattered less than the fact that it got done.

The financial arrangements that couples work out for themselves are not always conventional. In fact, I ran into some that were absolutely bizarre. But the motto is: "If it works for you, go with it." One working couple (he was a doctor and she an executive) had evolved a division of financial responsibilities during the early years of their marriage, and twenty-five years later the rules were still in effect. They had actually sat down and divided every household expense and allocated it to one or the other. He paid the rent and utilities, she paid for the food. She paid for the children's clothing, he paid for their schooling. She paid for the baby-sitter—unless it was for an evening devoted to one of his professional obligations, and then it was his responsibility. When they dined out, she paid, since she was responsible for the food. (Unless they were eating with his professional colleagues, in which case he picked up the tab!) The detail they had gone into to set up this arrangement was incredible, although they seemed to think it was perfectly normal.

"Why should he pay for everything when I make a very good salary?" she asked. When I mentioned to her the alternate possibility of pooling both incomes into one account and just paying all bills from that—in other words, regarding all earned monies as "ours" rather than "yours" and "mine"—she thought the concept ludicrous. "My money is my money, and his money is his money" she said firmly. And that was that.

My mother had a different theory: My father's money was their money and her money was hers. But, of course, she did not work and women of that generation often had to accumulate a hidden cache so that they would not have to clear every projected expenditure with their husbands. My father was unconcerned with the furnishing of the home and saw no reason why a couch ever had to be recovered, or a chair replaced, or a new piece of furniture be added. My mother, on the other hand, was always very house-proud and loved to redecorate the place from time to time. So she was forced to accumulate money from the weekly allotment that she received "for the table," which she did by shopping carefully, and used those savings for her sorties to the antique shops.

Whenever a new piece turned up in the living room, like a crystal hurricane lamp, my father would always ask, "What did that junk cost?" and my mother would always answer, "Twenty-five dollars." A nineteenth-century inlaid writing table—twenty-five dollars . . . a marble-topped coffee table—twenty-five dollars. It kept my father satisfied and my mother happy.

As I said before, the *only* criterion for a successful method of handling your finances is that it works.

The Power of Love

There's another vital ingredient that enters into the behavior patterns now—Love.

"What I call love now and what I called love when we first got married, they're not even close." Tim and Lois had married three years ago when they decided they liked the same things, had basically the same tastes, enjoyed being together, and were in love. Both thirty years old, they wanted to marry at this time and so they did.

Lois was pensive, soft-spoken and tended to evaluate her thoughts before pronouncing them, which conveyed an impression of slow-wittedness that was deceptive. Tim, ebullient and smart, was smitten with the gentle quality Lois emanated and deep down inside of him believed she was intelligent but not quite as bright as he, although she held a job of equal importance in the company where they both worked. The first three years of their marriage were filled with activity and stress as Tim added to his work load by matriculating for an MBA degree which he pursued at night, three times a week. Tense and tired, he was frequently short-tempered, which Lois handled with a hug and departure for another room. When he felt ready to talk, he would seek her out and tell her about the bitch of a day he had, and she would tell him about the goings on in her department. Many evenings were spent with little communication but just the comfort of knowing that the person you love is there. Gradually, a deep dependency developed between them and, with Tim, a tremendous respect for Lois. Beneath her quiet mien he began to discern a strength he had not suspected, and an instinctual ability to deal with people—a talent he was sorely lacking. They never seemed to have enough time together and he even resented the business trips he formerly adored, because it took him away from his wife and home.

Tim had entered the marriage with the expectation that he would provide the strength, the excitement, the familial direction, and Lois would go along with him providing back-up and comforts. But he had reckoned without the power of love to effect behavior changes. As his love deepened, so did his wish to please Lois, to make things easier and happier for her. His pre-marital concepts of male/female roles were forgotten as he began to insist that if she cooked dinner then it was only fair that he clear the table and do the dishes. Eventually the bachelor buddies with whom he had often gone out drinking stopped calling after he continued to turn them down. Evenings with them seemed trivial and uninteresting compared to time spent with his wife. Then one day at a seminar he was attending, the leader brought up the topic of friendship and asked the participants, one by one, "Who's your best friend?" And when it came Tim's turn, he answered unhesitatingly, "My wife."

My Wife/My Husband/My Friend

When Jeanette and Robert Lauer, professors at the United States University in San Diego, asked more than 300 veterans of long, happy marriages what had kept them together, one of the top items on the lists of both husbands and wives was, "My spouse is my best friend." In every interview I conducted, the final question was always the same:

"Who's your best friend?" No matter what facts and feelings the person tried to convey during our previous discussion, this came off as the truly significant summation of the marriage. About 90 percent of those I talked to answered instantly, almost automatically: "My wife," or "my husband." Many added, almost as an afterthought, as though the realization of the fact had just hit, "Of course," or "Absolutely." When the individual hesitated, thought for a minute or so, and then came up with a name, or "I don't really have any," then I knew that the marriage was not providing the partners with the benefits and pleasures implicit in a successful union.

"What is a friend? A single soul living in two bodies," said Aristotle. The sense of oneness that you feel as a married couple supplies a stability and comfort offered by no other relationship. Of course your spouse is your best friend, the person called first with news of your success or failure, of a problem or a pleasure. Who else cares more . . . who else's life and future is so intimately involved with yours? A friend can be sympathetic or supportive, but can never feel the level of concern of a spouse who shares the results of your emotions and life encounters on a day-to-day basis.

Trust: The Basic Ingredient

The trial period is over, this is the person you can trust and you must. During the Entry Level years of marriage, there is a withholding of self, a reluctance to reveal all for fear of reprisal or loss of love or respect.

"I can cry in front of my wife," one man told me.

"I feel free to be me because she won't trivialize it or use it against me as a sign of weakness. She understands where it came from and where it's all going and she cares because it's her life, too."

In her book *Married People,* Francine Klagsbrun noted that, "Trust . . . means you can open up to another person and not be hurt. In a good marriage there's so much trust that each partner can show his weakest side and know he'll still be loved."*

Developing trust in an "outsider" takes time. As children, we trust our parents implicitly but the person we marry has not always been part of the fiber of our lives and we hesitate to open up and make ourselves totally vulnerable to this unknown quantity. The operational word here is "outsider"; by now your spouse has become an "insider," your family, and you have learned to trust him/her. It is a great source of comfort to know that you have someone you can rely on to help you make decisions that are in your best interests. A woman said to me fervently, "I would trust my husband with my life," and that is exactly what you may be doing. Should you become ill or incapacitated in any way, this is the person who will be making your life-and-death decisions. When my husband underwent hospitalization for a serious illness, I spent many days in the Intensive Care Unit with other wives who were, like me, called upon constantly to make major decisions involving the patients' survival. Our husbands were able to use all their energies to fight against the disasters that had befallen them because they were fully confident that they could trust their wives to handle the medical crises that were beyond their control.

*New York: Bantam, 1985.

Situations involving trust do not always involve actual life and death, but they do affect the life or death of the marriage. One of the deep satisfactions of the marital condition is the sense of total security that comes from living with someone you believe in and who feels exactly the same way about you.

In interviews with more than 100 marital veterans, Francine Klagsbrun noted that they mentioned trust more than love. "Love was a given for them, but trust really says it all."

THE THIRD LEVEL

Parenthood?

A mother's pride, a father's joy.

—SIR WALTER SCOTT

Children begin by loving their parents; as they grow older they judge them; sometimes they forgive them.

—OSCAR WILDE

The "Yes" or "No" Decision

"Do I really want a child?" "Are we ready emotionally and financially?" "Is now the right time?" "How can we in good conscience bring another child into this rotten, over-populated world?" "Do I want to put my career on hold, possibly in jeopardy?" "Do we really want to give up our freedom? For what . . . look at all the problems you can have with kids."

If you have ever asked yourselves these questions, you are not alone. Every young married person I interviewed came up with, if not all, at least some of these reasons for agonizing over the decision to have or not have children. Whereas years ago, you-got-married-and-had-children was the accepted given in the life cycle, today's mores offer choices. But freedom, as always, carries with it the burden of decision-making. Before you just went along because it was the thing to do; you now have the right to suffer through the agonies of introspection, evaluation and analysis.

Sally and Dan had been married for six years,

had passed through some stormy days of Entry Level difficulties and were now comfortably and happily settled into a satisfying Acceptance Level routine lifestyle. Sally headed her own employment agency, a business she had built into a highly successful operation. Dan was a lawyer and had developed a busy practice which involved a good bit of travel. They enjoyed being with each other, they enjoyed being away from each other, they enjoyed their friends, they enjoyed their work, they enjoyed the financial freedom that enabled them to dine out often, to travel to exotic spots. They were sybarites who had the capacity and now the ability to enjoy life. Then Sally turned thirty-five.

A few days after her birthday, she was very quiet at dinner. "What's the matter?" asked Dan, who had become very adept at tuning into his wife's moods. "Don't you hear it?" She said. Dan listened for a few minutes and then said, puzzled, "Hear what? I don't hear anything." "The ticking of my biological clock," she answered.

Dan sat back. He knew what was coming and he did not want to face the discussion. "I'm thirty-five," said Sally. "If I want to have children, medical statistics show that I shouldn't wait much longer." "Do you want children?" asked Dan. "Do we want children?" he continued.

They talked until midnight. Sally admitted her own ambivalence because she knew that the major changes would be in her lifestyle, not Dan's. Bearing and caring for a child is the wife's responsibility and no matter how much the husband helps, the principal job is hers. Sally loved her work and was proud of the achievement of building a sizeable and highly lucrative business. How much would she have to give up if she became a mother? Was she willing to devote the time and energy to raising a child, and would it be as rewarding as her career had been? From Dan's viewpoint, their life was now perfect. Why risk it all for the unknown quantity of a child?

The next morning, after a very restless night, Dan announced to Sally: "Honey, I'm not much good with kids and I don't think I would relate to ours until he or she grew up into someone to talk to, but if you want a baby, it's O.K. with me. The decision is all yours." Sally was very moved by Dan's statement because she knew what it cost him, how much he loved his affluence and the high-flying lifestyle they had cultivated. Dan had grown up in a family that was poor in cultural, intellectual and financial resources. The taste for designer clothing, wines, ballet, opera, theatre and good food that was an innate part of his makeup was misunderstood and scoffed at by his parents. He had worked and taken out student loans in order to put himself through college and law school, and only now was beginning to reap the benefits. He relished the freedom to indulge his tastes and revelled in luxuries he had never had. For him to be willing to risk these gratifications was, to Sally, a superb testimonial of his love for her.

She spent the next week reviewing her feelings, analyzing the positives and negatives a child would bring to her, to Dan and to their life. Friday evening, she made her announcement: "I want to have a baby." And so, they did.

As I mentioned earlier in this book, you cannot run your life based on scoreboard tallies. Especially in the area of should or shouldn't you have children, where all the drawbacks are tangible and the benefits are intangible. The words "parental pride" and "satisfaction in creating and developing a good human being" make very sterile entries on paper. How can you fully explain the depth of pleasure these words convey? But all you have to do is to look at the faces of parents watching their child take his first steps, or perform in a school play, or graduate from school, and you know that powerful feelings are at work here that are primal and indescribable.

The question most frequently posed to me by young married women with careers is: "Do you think I should have children?" Since I have worked at a job throughout my marriage and have a daughter and made a reasonable success of both (in the case of my daughter, an unqualified superb success), I am regarded as somewhat of an oracle on the topic. I have a single answer: "In my opinion, you have but one life and you should try every experience life has to offer. Without question, parenting is one of life's most enriching experiences. Are you willing to forego it, and for what?" Today, with working mothers being the norm rather than the exception, the choice is easier to make. The child will not suffer (as mine did) from being the only kid on the block whose mother went to an office. Daycare centers are no longer just custodial; they often offer an enrichment and growth potential to children which was never before available. In fact, leaving a child at home with a domestic employee who tends to be neither educated nor intellectual is certainly less preferable than having the youngster spend the day with trained supervisory personnel who are at least verbal. This was learned by a doctor and her husband who could not understand why their two-year-old son was unable to communicate properly until their Jamaican maid went back home and they sent him to a daycare facility. Within a week, he was jabbering away, and they realized that he had previously spent his days with a loving but uneducated person who articulated basics only. How was the child to develop a vocabulary?

Can You Tell Me the Right Time?

In over 80 percent of the couples interviewed, it had been the wife who had pushed to have children. In some cases, the husbands had balked temporarily, usually with the excuse that "We're not financially ready to have a family," or "Wait until I am more established." Or most commonly, "This is not the right time." Most wives know that if they waited for the "right" time, their first child would arrive together with their first social security checks.

It is very difficult to evaluate the ideal moment for starting a family since everyone has different standards for what they consider optimum conditions for the onset of parenthood. Some will put it into purely economic terms: "We need a room for the baby . . . we need a house for a baby . . . we need a lot more money in the bank before we can think of having a family." Others will view the matter from a purely emotional standpoint: "I'm not sure that our relationship is really ready to accept a child into our life." Or sometimes just simply, "I don't feel like I'm ready to be a father." In most cases the wives' positive feelings were able to overcome the husbands' objections. Sometimes stronger measures were required.

"I just stopped using my diaphragm," one young woman told me. "I got tired of fighting with Tom about when is the best time for us to have a baby. I didn't tell him, of course. But when I got pregnant, I told him the truth. He was a little mad at first, but then he got so excited and thrilled about the idea of being a father that I could see he was glad I had made the decision for him. And of course, when the baby came, he was delirious."

Whenever I suggested this step of making the unilateral decision to cease contraception to women who were bemoaning their husband's constant procrastination of parenthood, their response was horror: "That's a breach of trust. I can't lie to my husband." But isn't his refusal to have children a betrayal of trust? Going on the assumption that most young men and women discuss their goals and dreams for life together before marriage, and agree that children are an integral part of the future picture, then his naysaying now is morally wrong.

"But he's not refusing to have children," the troubled young wives inevitably answer, "he just doesn't want them right now." The problem is that his "now," whenever it comes, may not coincide with her right time to bear babies. A man can go on having children for an unbelievably long time. Andrés Segovia, the famed classical guitarist fathered a son at 76. But fathering is merely fertilizing—that's the easy part. Although I think too much panic has been created about the importance of the biological clock for women, there is no question that the ability to conceive easily and carry through comfortably diminishes with the years. The husband who continues to give reasons to put off parenthood may be rationalizing away his wife's right to bear children, either consciously or subconsciously. As long as the wife knows that her husband truly wants children, a fact that was established before marriage, then all she is doing is adjusting the timetable.

One of the major forces at work in forming the decision to have children is the need to start one's own family in the face of the loss of parents. Young people do not dwell on their mortality—that's a preoccupation of the middle-aged and older. They tend to go along blithely with the expectation that everybody will be around always. Like Mom and Dad. And even Grandmother and Grandfather. Then a death occurs and suddenly the young sons and daughters realize that they can be abandoned and alone—that parents, aunts and uncles and all those people who contributed to the enjoyment of family holidays will not be around forever, and if they do not want to suffer watching the family circle diminish, they had better start creating some new members. As one man put it. "We have to make more of *us* because *they* are disappearing."

* * *

Emmett was an optimist. Everything always seemed wonderful to him and the future was cloudless. Why not? He had achieved everything he had set out to do when he entered college: got his MBA by age twenty-four, entered an executive training program with a large insurance company, was headed up the corporate ladder and at age thirty-two was happily married and living the classic Yuppie life. His wife, Virginia, who was thirty-one, talked from time to time about having children, but neither one felt too pressed to produce a family at the moment as they enjoyed vacations at Club Med, trips to Europe, bought any luxury that caught their fancy, and generally lived a life of total self-indulgence and pleasure-seeking. "Sure we want kids—but there's plenty of time," was Emmett's comment whenever the subject arose.

Then at eleven-thirty on a Tuesday morning his mother called from Green Bay, Wisconsin, to tell him that his father had dropped dead of a heart attack at his desk an hour ago. Emmett went numb with shock. There had been no warning, no telltale signs or illness. His father, who was only fifty-eight, had never been sick a day in his life. Emmett could not grasp the fact that this vital man he worshipped was gone. In Emmett's happy vision of life, nothing could happen to those he loved; they were invincible and indestructible, as was he. He had always imagined that his children would enjoy the same wonderful relationship with their grandfather as he had had with his. He looked forward to the pleasure and pride his father would take in Emmett's offspring, and the joy his father would get from taking his grandson to baseball games as he had his son. It was totally incomprehensible to Emmett that this could happen. That tall, strong wonderful man struck down . . . the person Emmett always called to discuss a particular business problem and could always depend upon to give him the right advice and help. Gone forever; the concept was inconceivable.

Emmett and Virginia flew to Green Bay immediately and stayed with Emmett's mother. He was shocked to see how sunken and frail she looked. The house was filled with relatives and friends. When Emmett commented on the absence of a close neighbor, he was told that he was in the hospital having a triple bypass heart operation. His sister was there, and he noticed how she and his mother kept clutching and cuddling her two-year-old son.

At the funeral, Emmett felt such a sense of grief and abandonment that he was almost overcome.

On the flight home, he sat silently looking out of the window and then turned to Virginia and said: "Let's have a baby." She was taken aback. "O.K. but why now? A child won't replace your father." "No, but it's time to start a new generation. And if my father could die, I know that I can too, and I don't want to leave this world without leaving something of myself behind."

The loss of a parent is hard at any age. I have heard it said that having children keeps you young. I think having parents is what keeps you young. As long as you have a parent extant, you are still the kid. Your parent treats you as a child, and that chicken-soup comforting is lovely at any age. We usually regard our parents as the supportive rock to turn to as we did in our growing-up years. When you are in your twenties and thirties, you accept your parents as indestructible—they are expected to be *there.* When the first one of them dies, the shock is shattering, not just because you lost someone you love, but because you suddenly undergo a change in life status as you realize that your position as nurtured child is disappearing. If you are not married at that time, you look to become so. If you are married, you start thinking about having children. It is the natural life cycle at work.

Should We Really Do It?

Joan and Roger had been married for fourteen years. I interviewed both of them in the lovely glass-walled room they had recently added to their house to take advantage of the breathtaking garden in front of us. Their two children, Jeffrey, aged ten, and Sybil, aged thirteen, were running happily in and out while we talked. "There was no question of having or not having children," said Joan. "We had talked about it before marriage and both felt that children were a major priority for us. In fact, I had seen Roger with our friends' small children, and I knew he would make a marvelous father. That was very important to me." We talked about the pluses and minuses of parenting and both settled back in their chairs and looked at each other to see who would start to answer my question: "Why did you feel you wanted children?" Roger said simply: "Because you want these small beings who love you totally and you love them totally. And there's the sense of heritage—I feel strongly about mankind being a continuation. I would love to go back in time to see my ancestors, in caves, in ships, wherever they were, and I want to know that I am continuing that cycle and leaving some of me here for always. I guess you could see it as ego, but I see it as a sort of immortality."

Joan said, "I always felt that having children was the most creative thing a woman can do. Bringing them up, passing on your values to them and watching them develop into what you hope is an extension of you—who will carry on, hopefully, in the ways you taught. That's wonderful. I know I could be out in the world, working, having a business, studying, but that would be only for me. My enjoyment comes from doing things for them, for my family. That's my happiness, to see others benefit and grow from what I gave them. That's my choice."

There are, of course, women who should not be mothers and men who should not be fathers. I have a number of friends who chose not to have children. (I hate the word "childless" because it unfairly infers that the childless person is less than normal. We start out with no children, their birth is an addition, and having none should not be presented as a subtraction.) They preferred to share their lives only with each other and did not feel the need or desire to introduce the unknown dimension of children to their already satisfactory existence. A few of them had miserable relationships with their mothers and suffered through what they saw as hateful childhoods and felt they never wanted to live through another mother-child relationship again, even though they would be in different roles. In all cases, the husbands went along with their wives. None appears to regret their decision: in fact, they confirm it by pointing out all the news stories about drugs and delinquency and are rather smug about all the anguish they have wisely avoided by choosing to not have children. I believe they are right . . . for them.

Today, there is a growing number of couples (and I interviewed quite a few of them) who have opted never to have children simply because they have worked out their career futures, his and hers, and feel that children will not fit into their plans. Not everyone has the strong desire to procreate, and there are many who have no interest in children or family life. Today women have unlimited horizons open to them and many get tremendous satisfaction out of their work, to a point that precludes the need for any other source of fulfillment. Since it is usually the wife who initiates the move to have babies, her refusal sets the pattern for the marriage.

In all the couples I have interviewed, I frequently encountered situations where wives convinced reluctant husbands to become fathers, and even where adamantly anti-family men were converted into enthusiastic parents by persistent spouses. But never did I run into a case of a husband who wanted children and was able to sway a wife who did not. The people who opted to skip parenthood were usually two-career couples who viewed their marriages as relationships of total parity that would be disturbed by the introduction of the responsibilities imposed by children.

* * *

Fran and Ed met while both were in college in California. He was the eldest of three children and she was an only child. They married after graduation and moved to Indiana, where Ed had a job offer. Fran had no particular career direction at the time—she had been a French literature major and teaching did not interest her—so she just followed Ed and cast about in their new town for some sort of work.

After five years, during which Ed had moved up in the company and Fran had tried a number of jobs, they decided it was time to assess their futures. As Ed put it, "We felt we had to make a seven-year plan for our lives at this time." They discussed their goals and analyzed what they really wanted out of life.

"Fran said she could never be the perfect corporate wife. In fact, she hated all the business socializing and having to be nice to some nasty jerk just because he happened to be my superior or customer. I respected her feelings and I thought about it and realized that I never wanted to be the president of this or any corporation. I liked my work, but

I didn't have that driving ambition and almost ruthlessness you need to make it to the top. I didn't like the cost that sort of thing exacted from an individual; being head honcho just wasn't that important to me." Then Fran came up with what was important to her. The job she had enjoyed most involved working with animals, and she decided she would like to become a veterinarian. They agreed that she should apply to schools to see if she could be accepted in a graduate program, knowing full well that it is even more difficult to get into veterinary schools than medical schools, since there are so few of them in this country. And if she did get accepted, Ed would find a job in that city.

To their delight, Fran was invited to matriculate in a fine school in Ohio, and Ed was able to find a position in a corporation located near the university. When I spoke to them, she was in her second year and they were both very busy and happy with their individual lives and life together. They bought an old house in a part of the city that was being gentrified and were enjoying the task of restoring it. Their social life consisted of university bashes and formal business dinners, which Fran sometimes managed to attend. "At exam time," said Ed, "I just keep out of the way. She gets impossible, so I work late or go out with some of my friends." Their life had evolved in a way that pleased and satisfied both, and they shared a relationship of absolute trust and mutual respect. "Some evenings she has a drink after class with some guys from school—and that's fine with me. There are times I have dinners with woman colleagues or customers or consultants, and that's O.K. with Fran." Their plans were to stay put until she obtained her degree and then move to wherever her job took her.

"I can always find a good job in my field," said Ed. "I mean, as long as I don't intend to make president, what's the difference which company I work for?" As for children, they both answered, "Not interested. Our parents are pulling at us to make them grandparents, but that's their problem. They'll just have to wait until my brother has kids." The way they see it, children and parenting have no allure for them and would only interfere with the lifestyle they have developed.

Ed has many interests—restoring the house, gourmet cooking—and Fran finds her work wonderful and exciting. They both love animals and have three dogs and two cats. Ed is highly thought of in his company, as he is capable and innovative and conveys that sense of certainty that emanates only from people who are secure and unafraid. Fran is near the top of her class. Someone once said that one needs three things to be happy: someone to love, something to do, and something to look forward to. The way Fran and Ed see it, they have it all.

The decision to have or not have children should be strictly a matter of personal choice determined only by a couple's own needs and feelings and not by any outside pressures, either from family or society. Societal pressures are trivial and family pressures are selfish. Just because your parents believe they would like to dangle a grandchild on their knees or have baby pictures to afford them equal time when friends haul out their grandchildren's photos are no reasons for you to have babies. Whatever arguments they present—like perpetuating the family name and line, or warnings about how lonely you could be in your declining years if you do not have offspring to provide comfort and succor—are merely their personal projections and may be totally invalid for you. As Ed told me: "I have no hangup about the need to reproduce myself or create and develop a human being. And I'm not so egotistical that I believe the world will in any way be diminished if I do not pass on my genes. As far as that bullshit I get from my father about carrying on the family name—who cares? And what happens if we have daughters? What's this great heritage he wants to pass along? As many generations back as I can trace, there hasn't been a single person of greatness, or anyone who made any contribution to mankind. For God's sake, we're not the Salks or the Mozarts. I have two brothers, one hasn't been able to get up early enough to look for a job for two years, and the other is a shoe salesman. The way I see it, the world will not suffer the loss of the continuation of our seed, and Fran and I have our lives and future going just where we want. We love each other, we're happy just as we are."

So much for family pressure. And as far as society is concerned, I remember that at my sixteenth birthday party a number of relatives and family friends made statements like: "Well, the next party we come to for you should be a wedding," thereby destroying the pleasure of the occasion with the insinuation of anxieties and pressures about the future. And then, right after my marriage, the next standard question was, "So when are you going to have a baby?" The full realization of the unimportance of these remarks came to me when I proudly told one of my parents' friends that I was to become a mother and she said, "That's nice, so what else is new?" I realized how all those years of questions that I construed as evidences of true concern were merely empty inanities, and how stupid I had been to allow idle remarks to affect the course of my life. None of those people gave a damn about whether or not I got married or had children; they were just making conversation.

The most sophomoric reason I have ever heard to not have children is the old bromide: "How can we be so irresponsible as to bring another child into this nuclear-threatened, polluted, over-populated world?" I would guess that many people reading this book will be surprised by my denigration of this seemingly noble rationale, especially those couples who believe the thought is original with them.

The first time I heard this statement was after World War II when my friend's older sister announced that she would never have children because how could she be so selfish as to bring a child into a world that would probably be destroyed by atomic bombs before the child reached puberty? Over the years, I have heard variations bringing it up to date with the latest world catastrophes, and always coming from purposeful young people who made the declaration with earnestness bordering on portentousness.

I once had to do research among archives of old newspapers of New York City dating back to the late nineteenth century, a pursuit I recommend to all those who bemoan the sad state of the world today and the horrifying evils that surround us now. If you were to change the date and masthead and type style of the old newspapers, any one of the front pages could pass for a current issue. Mayhem, rape, murder, assault, robbery, cruelty—they were just as prevalent then as now, even though many people choose to extol the simple virtues of the good old days. Yet mankind and the world have survived, and probably always will.

If people defer having children until the world is a better place to bring them up in, they will have a long wait. My answer to those who voice this concern is that if you fear for the condition of the world, then make your contribution to the improvement of this sorry state by creating good human beings who could work to possibly correct the ills that torture us all.

THE FOURTH LEVEL

Family

For man, the vast marvel is to be alive . . . My soul knows that I am part of the human race. . . . In my very own self, I am part of my family.

—D. H. LAWRENCE

The Birth & Afterbirth

The pregnancy time is exciting as you both become aware of the growth of your joint creation, and the birth is thrilling as your child emerges into the world. Now come the post-parturition blues, his and hers. Hers is expected, predicted and undoubtedly discussed by the attending obstetrician long in advance. But what about the displaced person—the husband? As one man put it: "For the first six to twelve weeks, you're not even there."

To give you a picture of the problem, let's go back to Sally and Dan.

* * *

Dan had thought that he could not relate to an infant and had stated so throughout Sally's pregnancy, but assured her that he would be a terrific father as soon as he and their child could communicate. The moment their baby daughter was placed in his hands, his resolve disappeared and the emotional bonding was instantaneous. Visiting Sally and the baby in the hospital was wonderful. Then they came home and their new life began.

Dan adored the baby, but after a few days he began to feel that while he had gained a daughter, he'd lost a wife. Although they had a nurse, Sally breast-fed the baby and was constantly involved with her care. When Dan came home from work, Sally barely kissed him hello and was then off to the nursery. "Why can't you take a half-hour to sit with me and have cocktails before dinner, like we used to? The baby's asleep, the nurse is here." He just could not understand her total preoccupation with the baby and her lack of interest in "his day." And her appearance! What happened to the attractive always well-groomed woman he was so proud of? She never seemed to wear anything but jeans and shirts with spit-up stains and her hair looked like it had been combed by an eggbeater.

Sally, on the other hand, could not understand her husband's impatience. Didn't he realize that caring for the baby consumed her? She who had dealt with formidable executives and tough business situations was riddled with inadequacy when faced with this tiny infant. What does she want? Why is she crying? What do I do now? Is there some instinctive ability in women to handle the needs of a baby that maybe I don't have? Every time the baby made a sound, Sally dashed into the room even if it meant leaving Dan in the middle of a sentence.

And their sex life—What sex life? Sally fell into bed every night totally exhausted, drained of desire and unable to cope with Dan's. He became resentful, angry and felt that he was in the way. He loved the baby and loved his wife, but wondered at times whether they had made the right decision.

Then one evening while they were eating dinner and he was telling Sally about a particularly important victory, she dashed away from the table because she thought she heard the baby cry. When she returned, he exploded. "For Christ's sake, you're becoming a crazy neurotic mother. You're beginning to hear things. What happened to that competent woman I used to be married to? Is this what the rest of our life will be like?"

Sally started to cry because she had her own doubts, too. They talked it out and realized that each one had to be aware of the other's needs and feelings. They had to help each other through this period.

This is a situation that only time and talking will resolve. Frequently the husband feels too guilty to complain about his resentment over loss of services. "What kind of monster am I, jealous of my own child?" It's perfectly natural for a man to resent the presence of this tiny being who has taken his wife from him. Where before he was the sole focus of her interest, someone else now gets top billing. The wife has a double problem—she has to cope with the baby and her husband. If the couple is fortunate enough to be able to reveal their fears to each other, time will smooth things over. It's worth it, because while they are fighting in the living room and bedroom, the baby in the other room is growing and changing every day in ways that will bring joyous wonder to the parents and will fill them with powerful emotions that will eclipse all other feelings.

Once they both relax in their new roles, other conflicts arise. Now that he's gotten over the fact that his wife cannot always share his pre-prandial cocktail with him, she becomes resentful that he's having the cocktail at all. "Why don't you ever change a diaper? You think only women are born with the aptitude to handle shit?" Then begins the battle over sharing responsibility for the baby's care. Many husbands automatically assume some jobs in baby care—they will take turns at getting up for the night feeding, if the wife isn't breast-feeding. They will gladly bathe the baby, pick her up when she cries. Some do not, because they feel inadequate and uncomfortable handling the baby and others because they view childcare as the wife's job.

There is no right and wrong here, merely accommodation to please each other. A woman who has been married for thirty-two years told me that she has never forgiven her husband for the fact that he was completely uninvolved with her children when they were infants even to the point of going out drinking with the guys some evenings to avoid the crying.

"Why didn't you ask him to help you?" I asked. "I couldn't," she said. "I was brought up to believe that taking care of the house and children was the wife's job—but I couldn't understand that if he loved me, how could he not want to ease things for me by helping. If he had pitched in voluntarily, I would have been in heaven, but I never thought to ask. And then when he came home from his bowling or drinking, he would get into bed and expect me to turn on for him. All I wanted at that time was some holding and affection, I was too tired for sex. But he just couldn't understand." When I asked her why she is still married to this man thirty-years later, she answered: "He's really a sweet guy and I love him and I know he loves me." "Since he has all this good stuff in him," I said, "don't you think he might have responded if you pointed out the inequities and injustices he was imposing on you? After all, he's a regular-Army man and he had those macho concepts. It probably never dawned on him that a husband should change a diaper." "You're probably right," she said. "I just never thought to ask."

The New Lineup

The "us" in your life used to be just the two of you but now there's a third party to be heard from . . . loud and clear. The addition of a child brings a new excitement to the household and new kinds of interaction. At the very beginning, it comes across as two-against-one because during infancy, the mother-child bond is intense and the father often feels helpless and useless. The more he participates in care of the child, the faster the happy threesome pattern will emerge. This progress is frequently blocked not by his own unwillingness to become involved but in the wife's unwillingness to permit it.

"She never lets me near the baby. I pick him up when he starts to cry, and if he doesn't stop in two seconds, she grabs him out of my arms and tells me I'm not doing it right. She just doesn't give me a chance to learn how to handle him."

I heard that complaint from young fathers almost as often as I heard young mothers comment acidly on their husbands' reluctance to deal with caring for the baby. New mothers have a very proprietary feeling about their babies that too often extends to the exclusion of the father. His own sense of ineptitude in handling an infant can be compounded by her impatience and criticism that can only serve to distance him from this new twosome and create resentments and jealousies that can be irreparable. At this particular time, it is important to establish a three-of-us relationship that will work to the benefit of the family forever.

The Green-Eyed Monster

"How could a parent be jealous of his own son?" asked my father of no one in particular as he walked out of a movie about the composer Johann Strauss. I was a small child at the time, but I remember vividly how exercised he became at what to him seemed inhuman. "A parent only wants what's best for his child. He gets only joy from the child's achievements. How could Strauss's father be jealous of his own son?" and he shook his head in disbelief.

But my father was speaking strictly subjectively. He was learned in the Bible, where sibling rivalry and fratricide was not unknown—witness Cain and Abel and Joseph and his brothers—but he was not a student of history, which is filled with royal sons who fled from assassins sent by their fathers. Nor did he himself ever encounter any situation where jealousy might have arisen, since my brother never entered his bailiwick.

A father's jealousy of his son is as common as the cold. Now that you fathers reading this book see these dread words in print, you can relax and stop feeling like some sort of horrific ogre just because you have experienced stabs of envy over the accomplishments of and/or attention given to your son by either the world at large or your wife. And you mothers out there, stop feeling ashamed because you resent your husband's adoration of your daughter, or get twinges of jealousy when you compare her size six figure to your size fourteen.

Why is it that "competition" is considered healthy and "jealousy" is regarded as sick? Why is "rivalry" looked upon as American as blueberry pie and Saturday footgall games and "envy" classified as repellent? They are all variations on the same words and the only thing to be concerned with is intensity.

In the first two interviews I conducted, I asked one wife if her husband had ever shown jealousy of her attention to their son and I got a fast, "Oh, never!" Then I changed the wording to, "When did you first notice your husband's little jealousies of your son?" and the answers were totally different. Very often she would ask wide-eyed, "You mean it's not just my husband?" and then be relieved to learn that many other women have encountered the same situations. After years of husband and wife being the sole recipient of each other's love and concern in the home, it is perfectly natural to feel some stabs of resentment when one sees one's mate lavish love and attention on a third party, even though it is their joint production. The situation only becomes a problem if either parent becomes fixated.

* * *

Blanche had been a highly successful executive and she and Evan had been married for ten years when they had their first child. They were both overjoyed with their infant son, and Blanche took a six-month leave of absence from her job in order to devote herself fully to the baby. And devote herself is exactly what she did. Morning, noon and night, the child came first. Unfortunately, he was diagnosed as hyperkinetic. He never slept through a night, and Blanche was always up with him. If he coughed, she ran for medication. If he cried, she picked him up. If he sneezed more than once, she called the pediatrician.

Evan felt displaced and disgusted. He tried to reason with Blanche, the pediatrician tried to reassure her that the child was basically healthy and did not warrant the excessive attention. But nothing could stop her obsession with the baby's well-being.

Evan loved Blanche and she loved him and they had established a solid basis for their marriage during the previous ten years before the birth of their son. That special caring and understanding enabled Evan to adjust to the new Blanche and the changes in her and their life together. He realized that their marital relationship would forever be different, but he was willing to accept it on the new terms. However, although he loved his son and enjoyed watching him grow and develop, he always felt jealous of the attention Blanche lavished on him.

In many homes, the husband and father comes first, but in their home it was the child. They were both very proud of their son's academic achievements—he was a bright student and always ran away with all the school honors. But Blanche never seemed as proud of her husband's professional growth, and when Evan's name appeared in the newspapers about special deals he had consummated, she was pleased but never as complimentary as she was to their son when he became the school valedictorian. It was only years later when their son joined Evan's firm and the two of them began working side by side that a new relationship developed between father and son, and the jealousy disappeared and turned into total pride. The respect the son showed to his father as he saw the intelligence and competence displayed made Evan blossom under filial admiration to which he was unaccustomed. For the first time in their lives, a special relationship grew between Evan and his son that excluded Blanche, a total turnaround from what had been. Evan was a very contented man: He was proud and pleased to have a wonderful son to share his working world and a wife whom he loved to share his home world. He felt it was all well worth the wait.

The problem with jealousy is that we are taught that good people share each other's joys as well as sorrows, and thus to be in any way less than happy at the good fortune of others is thought to be an indication of a character defect. *The Reader's Digest* once carried a homily about friendship that read: "A friend will sympathize with your failures. But only a good friend will sympathize with your successes." We regard jealousy as evil. If the jealousy is directed towards a member of your family whom you love, then you must be an abnormal monster. But that is so unrealistic, because in many situations jealousy is the normal instinctual reaction. And a small bit of it stimulates healthy competition.

Mothers who were beauties in their youth are bound to be a little envious of the sexual attractiveness of their nubile daughters at a time when they themselves suffer from the fear of waning charms. Fathers who were powerful tennis players will of course feel chagrined to be beaten on the courts by their young sons. That's all perfectly normal. Things only get out of hand when the mother becomes coquettish with her daughter's boyfriends, laboring under the assumption that her superior allure will win out. Or the father drives himself obsessively to beat his son, refusing to face the foregone edge of the power of youth over age.

Electra and Oedipus may have been characters of legend, but cases of daughters overly attracted to fathers and sons being abnormally drawn to mothers, as well as the reverse, appear often in the annals of psychiatric journals.

What I am trying to convey here is that some jealousy among family members is natural; it is only excesses which create dangers. If parents notice that their mates are rankled by attentiveness to their children, it behooves them to evaluate their behavior carefully. If it is indeed excessive, what are the reasons? And if it is not, what are the reasons for the spouse's overreaction? This is a situation that calls for discussion and perhaps outside help. Jealousy in small doses can be harmless or even constructive, but in large doses it can be destructive.

Where's Daddy?

You may well decide to stop having children after one child, or go on to have a second or third or even more. The apartment quickly becomes too small, the kids have no place to play, so it's off to a house in the suburbs. It's beautiful, it's spacious, it's mortgaged and it's located a distance away from the workplace. Which brings new elements into life.

George Bernard Shaw said that it was too bad that youth was wasted on the young. It's also too bad that financial security is usually the province of the old, because the time of bringing up children customarily coincides with the struggling-up-the-ladder time when working hard and working late is necessary for the building of a future. If the wife has elected to stay at home with the children, she has to expect many evenings of a weary husband arriving home way past the children's bedtime who may fall asleep during her recitation of the day's family activities.

A matrimonial attorney I spoke to told me that she sees many women who come to her at this stage of their marriage and want to file for divorce.

"They don't really want a divorce. They just have some unrealistic fantasy of what life should be, with the husbands bounding through the front door at 5:30, going out into the backyard to toss a ball with the kids, coming back in and having cocktails as she regales him with the adorable things the children did that day and he tells her about the exciting deals he has consummated and then the whole happy family gets to sit down at the table together like Ozzie and Harriet and the Waltons.

"The reality is the guy has had a bitch of a day taking all kinds of shit from customers, clients, bosses and worrying about keeping his job or the business from going under, and then he has to take a one-hour commute and all he wants to do when he gets home is take off his clothes and empty his head. He'd love to be there in time to help the kids with their homework so they'll get good grades and get into good colleges, but he has to fight out there to be sure he makes enough money to pay the tuition. Rationally and logically his wife knows that he must work hard to pay the bills and build their future. In fact, if he didn't she might think less of him. But somewhere deep in her subconscious she sees his latenesses as rejection of her and their family. And also down in that same submerged psyche is jealousy of his more exciting world while she's confined with monosyllabic finger-painters all day. So she starts to nag him:

"If you really cared about me and the kids, you'd make it your business to be home some evenings on time. All I ever hear from the kids is 'Where's daddy?' You never spend time with them." And then she throws in about how he plays tennis on the weekends instead of spending time with the family. The poor bastard plays tennis from eight to ten Saturday mornings to let off steam and keep fit, and she makes him feel like a deserter. The next thing she tells him "We don't communicate any more." I think that word "communicate" should be struck from the language. When I hear the word in my business, it usually comes from the wife and means, "I want to talk and he'd better listen."

When I asked her how she counsels a woman who comes to her with these problems, she said with a rueful smile, "I tell her to go out and get a job."

This is a rocky period for young families, since there's right on both his and her side. Usually when a wife accuses her husband of not spending enough time with their children, she is not so much complaining about the children's deprivation as her own and the fact that she alone is bearing the burden of child-rearing. There are no solutions to these problems, only adjustments and reconciliation to the givens of the situation. A young man working to build a secure future for his family has to devote a good deal of time and emotion to the task, a fact that his wife must recognize. On his side, he must evaluate his expenditures of time . . . are these career demands really important or is he merely using them to avoid some familial responsibilities or because he finds the workworld more exciting than the homefront? If she accepts that his workload is unavoidable and still resents the isolation, then it's time she consider getting a job, either part- or full-time, so that she, too, can have some of the stimulation of the outside world.

When both husband and wife are working, a different set of problems emerges. Now two exhausted people arrive home at the end of the day to be greeted by the excited child or children who want to tell about everything that occurred that day within the first five minutes. Both parents would love to first shed clothing, take a shower, have a drink, whatever they need to relax. Usually one of them does—daddy.

A woman who is a physician and is married to a physician told me, "If a husband and wife are performing surgery together, it's the wife who will suddenly remember during the operation that their home is out of toilet paper." The fact is that domestic chores are still the wife's department and no matter how much the couple tries to maintain equality at home, she tends to be more equal than he. If this issue is not confronted, more and more responsibilities will accrue to her and inevitably an explosion will occur. Assignments should be allocated. ("I'll feed the kids, you bathe them." "I'll cook dinner and you clean up.") During the entire thirty-four years of my marriage, I walked away from the table after every meal. It just evolved, without any discussion, during the beginning of our marriage that since I prepared and cooked the meal, my husband felt he should assume the task of cleanup.

This is a rough time in the marriage, but also an exhilarating one. Everything is growing, everything is ahead, you're both filled with dreams and plans for your and your children's future. Watching your offspring develop into individuals is marvelous. "Children add dimension to our life and marriage," a young father told me. "We just took them, aged four and two, on a trip to England. I've been there before, but seeing it through their eyes was a totally different and wonderful experience. You know, it was my vacation and I never once thought of spending it without them. Vacation to me means relaxation and pleasure, and that means spending the time with those you love."

Doing things as a family, going on outings and trips is great fun, albeit frequently wearing when the kids are toddlers. "We do lots of things together now because we know that when they get to be teenagers they won't want to spend time with us, and I'm not sure that we'll want to spend a lot of time with them. And I think that's how it should be," said one mother of three.

This doesn't preclude your going on second-honeymoon vacations from time to time. It is not a betrayal of familial devotion to want to return to romanticism and get off together and be husband and wife instead of Mommy and Daddy once in a while. In fact, it makes you better at the job of parenting. The man who told me about taking his family to England also mentioned that for his wife's fortieth birthday, he surprised her by coming home Thursday evening with two tickets to Bermuda and all arrangements made with his mother to take care of the children for the weekend. Undoubtedly many women reading this book will say enviously, "My husband doesn't even remember to send me flowers!" Don't be bothered. If the love and caring and happiness together are there, it will show up in other ways.

Growing Children, Growing Problems

From the first day your child steps into a daycare center, a nursery school, day camp, kindergarten—you are no longer in total control. Other authority figures enter the scene and new factors come into positions of influence and you see your child change, often into someone unfamiliar. This process that continues all during the growing years brings conflicts on the home front as husband and wife respond differently to the challenges presented by the developing youngster.

* * *

Maryanne was weary of the fight she and Donald were going through again. "So what if Tommy wants to wear an earring?" she said for the tenth time. "He's doing fine in school, so if this is how he wants to rebel, what's so bad?" Donald was in the fury he always worked up to when he saw his fourteen-year-old son slouch off to school dressed in the usual jeans, shirt and earring. "Because he looks like a freak!" answered Donald. As she cleaned away the breakfast dishes, Maranne said calmly, "Webster's definition of a freak is a thing that's very irregular and unusual. Since half the boys in his class wear an earring, you must be wrong."

During the early years of child-rearing, Maryanne and Donald agreed perfectly on most issues. Discipline, bedtime, responsibilities about cleanup and room care—these were basic home rules their son and daughter abided by with no difficulties. But adolescence brought far more complex problems about which the parents did not always see eye-to-eye.

It is surprising to get an unexpected reaction from someone you felt you knew well; it is shocking to get a totally unpredicted response from the person you thought you knew best—yourself.

Donald was a picket-carrying protester in the sixties and saw himself as liberal and open-minded. To his bewilderment, his attitudes towards his children's behavior was, as Maryanne put it, "hard hat conservative." Suddenly Maryanne and Donald found themselves quarreling often, sometimes to the point of one or the other's storming out of the house. And it was always about the children. Their home became a battlefield with clearly defined sides, Maryanne and the children against Donald. The bitterness began to spill over into all areas of their relationship as husband and wife. Their sex life became a mix of the desultory and the mechanical, and worse, the easy affection they had always displayed towards each other disappeared, including the goodnight kiss that had been their custom always.

Then one day Donald came home early and was sitting in the living room when his wife and daughter walked in laughing together. "Well, where have you two happy ladies been?" he asked with a smile. And before she could think, his daughter answered, "The gynecologist." "What's wrong?" he asked in alarm. Maryanne took a deep breath and said, "Nothing's wrong. Sally was fitted for a diaphragm." Donald stood up and his face turned red with fury: "For God's sake—she's only sixteen. Are you trying to turn her into a whore?"

A screaming match ensued with Donald hurling horrible accusations at Maryanne's competence as a mother and dire predictions about the moral state of Sally's future. The episode ended with Sally running to her room crying hysterically and Maryanne sobbing quietly in the living room. When he calmed down, Donald was shaken with self-recrimination and remorse.

"What the hell's happening to me?" asked Donald. "I just went crazy, didn't I? Why?" "That's a good question," said Maryanne. They began to talk and talk and talk until it finally came out that as a child of the sixties Donald had memories of friends who had self-destructed on rampant drugs and sex and was abnormally fearful of such a fate for his children. They brought the children in on the discussion so that they, too, would understand the demons that were driving their father. The situation did not resolve itself overnight, but it was the start that put them all on the way of respecting each other's point of view and learning to live with it.

The irreplaceable elements that children bring to a marriage are the love, pleasure and pride shared by the parents unmarred by any conflicting emotion. A major happiness factor missing from second marriages is the ability of partners to share with their spouses the joys produced by children of a previous marriage without encountering some jealousy and disinterest. Children can also produce a great deal of pain and disputation that can lay heavy stress on the marriage. But when you come down to it, it's a cause in common between husband and wife that each comes to with the deep and pure love of a parent, so its damaging effect on a marriage is usually temporary. And like all the ordeals suffered together during the connubial years, these experiences bind rather than break the relationship. If you two can live through the adolescent years of your children, you can survive anything. But you have to be sure that the friction between you has really been caused by the child's behavior and not by some deeply rooted personal dissatisfaction.

* * *

Mike walked in the front door and dropped his garment bag and attaché case on the floor, exhausted from a three-hour trip from Cleveland which should have taken one hour. That came on top of a day of aggravating meetings that included the firing of two salesmen. All he wanted at the moment was a hot shower and a drink. As he headed for the bedroom he shouted "Hi, I'm home." His wife, Annette, came out of the kitchen and said angrily:

"Barbara was on the phone for three hours last night with that turkey of a boyfriend! *If* you were trying to call me, that's why you couldn't get through."

Mike sighed. "First place, whatever happened to 'Hi, honey, glad to have you home and did you have a good day?' Secondly, I didn't call you because I didn't get back to my room until after midnight. And third, I just walked in, for God's sakes, what do you want me to do, take Barbara out to the woodshed? She's sixteen years old. How about you exerting a little discipline? You're her mother, why didn't you make her get off the damned phone? And how about showing a little consideration before you hit me with all your problems." And he stormed off to the bedroom.

"*My* problems?" Annette yelled as she followed him. "She's your daughter as well as mine. How about you getting involved with raising her instead of running all around the country having a good time with your expense account dinners and God-knows-what-else."

Mike spun around and said in tight-lipped fury: "If you got yourself involved in something worthwhile instead of just shopping and gossiping with those dipshit friends of yours, maybe you wouldn't be so jealous and angry every time I get home from a trip." And he slammed the bathroom door.

Annette sat down on the bed, utterly devastated. She knew her husband had just hit on a truth that was really bothering both of them but had never before been said. Mike and Annette were married when she was eighteen and he was twenty-two. He had just completed service in Korea, they met on a blind date, fell in love and decided to get married because that was what you did then. The first few years were a struggle as Mike went to college under the G.I. Bill and held a full-time job at the same time. Annette worked for a while but then she became pregnant with their first child and quit work, which was also what you did then. Mike finished college, got a good job with a major manufacturing company in the area and then went on to complete his MBA at night.

He was capable, hard-working and ambitious and had moved steadily up the management ladder and she was proud of him. But she began to sense that he wasn't proud of her and her lack of education and intellectualism. She felt inferior, inadequate and left behind. She noticed Mike's annoyance when she sat mute at company functions because she feared making a gaffe. She knew he was irritated when he saw her reading Sidney Sheldon or Judith Krantz instead of the books on politics, biography or history that he preferred. He had hinted many times that, now that the children were in their teens and somewhat self-sufficient, she ought to develop an interest outside of the home. Annette knew that he was right, but she was paralyzed with insecurity and unable to take any steps to pull herself out of the morass of self-hate. She was also wise and honest enough to admit to herself that her unreasonable anger at Mike when he returned from business trips was based on envy of his achievements and fear that he was growing farther and farther away from her.

After Mike showered and changed, she had his martini and some nibbles waiting on the coffee table. When he emitted his first sigh of pleasured relaxation, she said "You're right. Let's talk."

When Mike and Annette married seventeen years earlier, their basic reason was because they were in love. As a matter of fact, in a 1985 American Women's Opinion Poll reported in *USA Today*, 83 percent of the 3,000 women and 1,000 men asked why they marry gave being in love as the prime motivation. But couples who are in love usually take the time to get to know each other before they plunge into marriage, which is something Mike and Annette failed to do. Mike was fresh out of a war and eager to get on with his life, and having a wife seemed like the right move. Annette's basic training, like all young women of her time, was to get married and have babies and live happily ever after. Neither one questioned their congruence of interests or goals but merely accepted that physical attraction plus similar backgrounds were sufficient bases for marriage. Their early years together were so hectic, with Mike virtually working around the clock and two babies coming one after the other, that their relationship was strictly fulfillment of the basics, like food, sex and money. Who has time to discuss the philosophy of life and the universe when you're scrambling to survive? Evaluation of emotional needs is a luxury that can be indulged in only when financial needs are no longer a problem.

When they became secure and Mike was flourishing in a company that encouraged its executives to find out what they did well and then permitted them to do it, he began to seek a level of companionship from his wife that he never before demanded. When it came to parenting and running the household, he had always found Annette sensible and capable. Her judgment was good and she was absolutely dependable, which he appreciated and valued. Their sex life was fine, although no longer too exciting, but sufficiently satisfactory to prevent his seeking solace elsewhere. He had thought of it, but his own sense of morality and the closeness they had developed over the years precluded any extramarital activity.

"I just couldn't do that," Mike explained. "I know that if I had slept with another woman, Annette would know it the moment I walked through the door." But his hard-fought-for college degrees had made him aware of the value of education, and he began to note Annette's lack of knowledge and interest in matters other than the mundane and domestic. Compounding the difficulty was that many of the women of Annette's age he was meeting in business were bright, aware and stimulating and he found himself comparing them to his provincial wife. The situation was especially irritating when he came home on a high after a particularly exhilarating trip, where his presentation had been met with effusive commendation, and his exuberance was dampened instantly by Annette's greeting him with some carping domestic complaint or story about what he viewed as petty nonsense. At moments like that, he longed for an interested companion with whom he could share his triumph, who would understand the details of the part of his life that was so important to him.

When Annette said, "You're right. Let's talk," it was the perfect opening to a discussion for which they were both ripe and ready. Aided somewhat by the repression-releasing effects of their martinis, an outpouring of revelation and reaction began.

"You say I put you down when you come home full of yourself and what great things you did?" said Annette. "I'm an amateur when it comes to put-downs compared to you. You should see your face when I tell you some of the things that happened around the house while you were away. You get that same look you get when I serve boiled cod for dinner. But what else do I have to tell you? Nothing exciting happens here—things just go on day by day. Don't you think I'd like to greet you with some bit of fascinating news like I just discovered the cure for cancer? Sure I envy your life—it sounds so glamorous and exciting staying at hotels, eating in fancy restaurants, sending your clothes out to be pressed, calling room service when you want a snack, talking to interesting people. With me, it's cottage cheese for lunch and tuna casserole for dinner, and cooking and washing dishes and cleaning the house and yelling at the kids to clean up their rooms or do their homework. You get all these people telling you how great you are. The last compliment I got was when old Mrs. Gibbons next door told me how pretty my kitchen curtains looked when I washed them last week. When you come back from a trip, you're either all hyped up or dragging-your-ass exhausted. So what do you want from me? A pat on the back when you're up and a soft comforting shoulder when you're down? Who does that for me, ever?"

Mike agreed that maybe his expectations were somewhat unfair and unreasonable. Then he sat there, twirling his martini glass and wondering how to word his recommendation tactfully.

"Honey," he said slowly, "If you find your life dull, why don't you try to do something with it. I mean like get a job. Something that gets you out of the house, something that gives you some self-esteem."

"But what can I do? I'm not qualified for anything."

This was what Mike had been waiting for. "Then why don't you go back to school and get your degree?"

Annette had been sitting on the edge of her chair and she fell back and was silent for a full minute.

"That's really what this is all about, isn't it? That's what you've wanted all along. A college-educated wife. You're ashamed of me, aren't you?"

Mike smiled ruefully. "*In vino veritas*. Yes, you're right. It's not that you're dumb—you're one of the smartest people I know. You're quick, you're intelligent. It's just that you're uneducated, and that makes a difference in your whole outlook on life, your sense of yourself. Look, you helped put me through school, now it's my turn to do that for you. The kids are independent, they don't need you that much any more. It's time you did something for *you*."

Annette matriculated that semester in a local college and discovered when she took Psych I that she had a natural talent for psychology and she loved it. She completed her major at the top of her class and was given a scholarship for a master's degree in social work in a major university within driving distance from home. When she went up to the podium at graduation to receive her degree with honors, Mike's eyes were filled with tears of pride. Now when Annette accompanied him to business affairs or dinners, his colleagues told her that Mike did nothing but boast about his achieving wife. The entire configuration of their relationship changed as they developed a mutual respect for each other.

How many times have you heard people discussing a couple who had divorced because he grew and she didn't, or the other way around? But that's really nonsense, because we all grow in some manner or another as we go on living. Annette was more mature than she had been when first married, and her capabilities to handle the household, including all the family finances, had certainly developed. She had grown, but not in the one specific area that was extremely important to her husband. He was an education snob which prevented him from valuing anyone who did not have a degree. She could have taken the position that his attitude was petty and shallow, as it certainly was, but what would that have achieved?

There will always be points in a marriage where one partner takes a stand that is utterly unreasonable and immovable because of emotions beyond his or her control. It is important that the spouse recognize a stone wall situation and realize that his or her only choice is not to judge but merely to deal with it. "I stuck to my guns because I knew I was right" is an epitaph for marriage. In this case, Annette knew that the need for his wife to have a college education was so basic to Mike's image of himself that she must either win a degree or lose a husband. Fortunately, she had the desire, drive and ability for the task, and in the long run his neurosis brought her great benefits.

When There's a Will, There's Not Always a Way

When you have children you must of course draw up a will. The insurance company advertisements remind you that you must provide for your family, as they put it euphemistically, "when you're not there," and that applies both for saving money and arranging for the handling of it, which means a last will and testament.

It's hard enough to get ourselves to take care of this important legal arrangement, because deep down inside we feel that by arranging for our deaths we are tempting the fates, and if we ignore the whole thing, maybe it will never happen. But we all know this is unrealistic and usually most couples get around to making out their wills at some point after their children are born.

It would seem that all should be cut and dried here, because all that you both own will of course go to your children, so why am I bringing up this topic at all in a book that is aimed at preparing you for the normal marital tribulations that occur? In truth, making out your will can be the cause of the biggest fight you may ever have in your entire marriage.

"Who gets custody of your children should you both die in a joint demise?" This seemingly minor question that is routinely posed by the attorney will invariably create a major conflict between husband and wife.

"Are you kidding? Your brother raise my kids? I wouldn't trust him with a parakeet. Forget it."

"I suppose you think your sister would do a better job? The only things she loves are herself and her Mercedes. I'd never let my children be brought up in that loveless intellectual wasteland."

"Then what about my parents?"

"Your mother would feed them to death and your father would bore them to death. How about my parents? I turned out O.K."

Long meaningful silence.

Who gets custody of your children if you are not here is one of the most difficult decisions you'll ever have to make. Fortunately, this is a clause that rarely has to be invoked, but you must prepare for the possible eventuality. All parents feel that only they are qualified to bring up their children and shudder at the idea of their beloved offspring being raised by anyone else. Especially since most parents tend to be critical observers of the way other people handle their families. The idea of one's sister-in-law or brother-in-law, whom we chronically disparage, being entrusted with the tender psyches of our offspring is a horrifying thought and very difficult to face.

Some parents misguidedly choose to assign guardianship to friends, with whom they of course have discussed the possibility. But unless it's a very close and devoted friend, the result would undoubtedly be that, should the unthinkable occur (and that's how most friends regard the probability of you and your spouse dying simultaneously), they would turn the children over to your family anyway. The reality of introducing someone else's small children into your home and being totally responsible for their upbringing is quite different from a hypothetical discussion. You may not adore your in-laws, but at least they are family and would give your children love and a strong sense of belonging rather than being unwanted outsiders.

So fight it out and then make the commitment. It will probably never happen anyway.

THE FIFTH LEVEL

R & R

(Rebirth [hers] Reconciliation [his])

. . . there is a dark
Inscrutable workmanship that reconciles
Discordant elements, makes them cling
  together
In one society.

—WILLIAM WORDSWORTH

"I'm Free, Says She"

The kids are in school and can bicycle or drive to their extracurricular activities; she is released from major familial caretaking responsibilities. "I'm free . . . now it's time for ME," she says. "I'm still young, competent, sexy—where do I go from here?"

If she put her career on "hold" during the child-rearing years, it is now time to pick up where she left off. If she had no profession or career or is no longer interested in the work for which she was trained, it is now time for her to explore the various paths of entry or re-entry into the working world.

Years ago, such options did not exist for women and the over-forty female who sought a job ended up behind the counter of a department store if she was lucky. Today maturity is often valued above youth when it comes to evaluating qualifications for a job requiring judgment and responsibility. In fact, discrimination due to age or sex is illegal. And there are all those women's studies programs offered by universities that are aimed at equipping re-entry women to make the transition from kitchens to careers. There's a whole exciting world out there for her and the possibility of setting out on a new self-gratifying path gives her a sense of anticipation and exhilaration that is heady stuff, indeed.

That's great for her. But what about him? Her rebirth couldn't come at a worse time because he's about to head into his midlife crisis, the male menopause. It's a rough period that can hit crisis proportions in their marital relationship.

Adjusting His Dreams Downward

The Peter that came home every evening had become unrecognizable to Carol. Where was the exuberant man who started talking before he had his coat off, who headed for the children's rooms to say "Hi!" before he went in to shower and change into jeans and an old sweater and then chatted in the kitchen with her while she put the finishing touches on dinner preparation?

For the past month, he seemed to slip into the house, head for a drink after he changed, and then sat mute at the dinner table while the kids babbled away about their day's doings. Family life swirled about him, but he was no longer a participant. He was a zombie, totally sapped of enthusiasm or interest in anything. This paralysis extended into a major area of their marriage—sex. Not only had he become totally disinterested in making love, but the one time he did make the attempt, he was mortified to find that he was impotent.

Carol tried to talk to Peter about the roots of this depression that had gotten a hold on him, but he refused to discuss it. "I'm fine. Leave me alone. I'm just tired." And when she attempted to bring it up again, he went into an uncharacteristic rage which shocked her.

"Peter, this can't go on. We have to talk. Or you've got to go for help. Or we have to go for help. I don't like what's happening to us."

What was happening to Peter is he had reached the age and stage in life where he had to come to terms with who and what he is and reconcile this reality with the dream of what he might have been.

When we are young, we create blueprints for our future, what we plan to achieve and ultimately become. Little boys are taught to go forth and conquer the world. Thus big boys, men, have to accept the fact at some time in their lives that they will never attain those illusionary goals.

Peter had just come to realize that he would never be the chief executive officer of the Fortune 500 company he worked for, just as other men must realize they may never become President of the United States, or build financial empires or even own their own gas stations. Now is the time for all good men to adjust their dreams downward and revise their blueprints of the future into the solid realities of today.

Peter had much to be thankful for. He had a secure middle management position in a large company with all the attendant benefits that insured his and his family's future. He owned a lovely house, had a happy marriage and three nice children. But his forty-fifth birthday came about the same time he was passed over for a promotion that would have moved him from the departmental to the corporate level, and he was coming to grips with his actual achievement potential. He had to suffer through the painful period of introspection and reevaluation of self, as well as the readjustment of his goals and dreams. Unfortunately, one of the concomitant effects of stress and loss of self-esteem is loss of sexual drive and sexual performance ability. This kind of temporary impotence has the discouraging effect of feeding upon itself: he thinks less of himself as a man in the marketplace and then is a bust in bed, which proves that he is less of a man everywhere. It's insidious and hell to live through for husband and wife. During this trying period, she can do almost nothing right. If she's sympathetic, he thinks she's condescending. If she's understanding, he accuses her of hypocrisy: "Don't give me that 'I know how you feel' crap. You don't know anything." If she tries to get him to talk about his feelings and makes any comments, he blows up: "One lousy psych course in college and that qualifies you to put out a shingle as a psychiatrist?"

Every wife who has survived her husband's midlife crisis shudders at the recollection. But it will pass. Sometimes time and his own strength, plus his wife's patience, gets them through it. Sometimes the help of a therapist is needed. But eventually he comes to realize that whatever and whoever he is now, that's the person he will be forever. And you know what? All things considered, that ain't half bad!

But now let's get back to her, and how the new "her" can affect the old "him." If she goes back to school, either to acquire or complete a degree or perhaps learn a whole new discipline to set her off on a new career, her husband will be proud and delighted—while she is in school. Of course, he may grumble at the slapdash meals and microwaved leftovers and diminished services, but usually these complaints are half-hearted because everyone respects education. And best of all, a wife in school is totally non-competitive to a man in business.

But what happens if she enters his arena and becomes successful?

Role Reversal

Eric was always called "brilliant." The top 700's in his SAT's, National Merit Scholar, Ivy League college on early admission, the world awaited him. Ellen and he met while she was an undergraduate at Boston University and he was taking his MBA at the Harvard Business School. They married upon her graduation and she became a speech pathologist, for which she had trained, and Eric embarked upon a career in marketing for a major advertising agency. He moved ahead quickly. They soon bought a house in an affluent suburb and Ellen retired to raise their family. By the time their last child entered high school, Eric had changed jobs five times. He moved from one high echelon position to another, but never seemed to raise himself above a specific level.

Eric had a brilliant facile mind and a sharp intolerance and impatience for those who didn't. At meetings, he grasped the significance of a problem instantly and came up with elegantly conceived solutions that everybody admired. But neither his colleagues nor superiors admired the condescension with which he treated all those who either did not see or did not agree with his conclusions. His handling of business analyses was brilliant, his handling of people was abysmal. Every major advertising agency wanted him to head their marketing department, but none wanted him to head their company.

Eric had never learned that although superior scholastic credentials make you immediately acceptable for high positions, there are far more important qualifications required to reach the top, like the ability to deal with and lead people, which requires an understanding of human nature and motivation. He had just left his last job when the position as executive vice-president went, once again, not to him but to someone whom Eric regarded as his mental inferior. Each move made him angrier and more frustrated.

It was at this time that Ellen decided to go back to work. Never having really liked speech pathology, and having heard all these years about Eric's field, she applied for and got an entry-level job as the assistant to the marketing manager of a small company that planned to produce and market home-care products. Eric treated Ellen's sortie into commerce as a harmless pursuit to which he had no objection so long as it did not interfere markedly with their home and family life. In fact, he enjoyed the new novelty of traveling to work together with his wife.

During her first year as working wife and mother, some minor adjustments were made and everything went smoothly. Meanwhile the company Ellen worked for grew tremendously, and her job entailed more and more responsibility. Then her boss quit and, without consulting Eric, she worked up the nerve to walk into the president of the company to ask for the just-vacated position. And she got it. Eric's reaction to the announcement that his wife was now the marketing manager of a multi-million-dollar company was complete shock. He was congratulatory and, on the surface, supportive. But during their champagne and dinner celebration, Ellen could detect underlying conflicts that she both expected and dreaded but decided to ignore with the hope that they would resolve themselves in time.

Ellen's career burgeoned as it was discovered that she had a remarkable talent for evaluating what products would sell, and in motivating company personnel to sell them. She flew all around the country to address meetings, and began getting written up in the very trade papers that were read in Eric's industry. She was riding high and came home every evening filled with details of her activities that she would want to tell Eric. But his reaction was either total lack of interest or condescending condemnation of how ineptly she and her company had handled the situation. All he wanted to talk about was the rampant stupidity he saw around him every day in his office, what idiots he had to deal with and what was the point of giving them his insightful advice if no one had the brains to take it. His bitterness grew and he began to slide into a depression.

Then one Friday he came home and announced that he had not only quit his job but his career. No longer would he suffer the interference of fools but would start his own business where he could control events and make a fortune based solely on his ability and no longer be deterred by the inadequacies of others. Financing for this new venture would come from the pension fund payment that was now due upon his resignation. Ellen was aghast: this was the money they had planned to draw upon for the children's college education. She was well aware of the risks of starting a business, and even more conscious of her husband's inability to deal with the nitty-gritty details that such an enterprise demanded. But Eric was so excited and enthusiastic at the prospect and filled with the kind of electric optimism she had not seen him exhibit since his Harvard days, that she felt she must let him take the plunge.

The first months of Eric's search for the right business were wonderful for him as he was buoyed with hope and his days were filled with phoning, reviewing potential prospectuses and seeing people. Since his activities were home-based, he took over many of the household chores that Ellen had previously performed, such as food shopping and dealing with the various maintenance problems that arose. But soon it became apparent that he could find nothing that pleased him, and they were rapidly going through their savings and he started getting angry and depressed once more.

Now the children were becoming involved as they began to perceive their father as a different figure. "Why is he always hassling us to do things? Why doesn't he go to work like other fathers and leave us alone?" They found difficulty in adjusting to this new parental lineup—father at home and mother the breadwinner, especially since he had always been such a strong and dominating persona in the home. They were often frightened at his tirades usually about some petty detail like leaving a milk container on the table. Frequently when Ellen arrived home in the evening she found herself in the role of referee between Eric and one of the children.

Ellen and Eric had always enjoyed sex together. Early on in their relationship they had been free enough to instruct each other on techniques that each needed or preferred and their sex life was highly satisfactory. But now the bedroom became a battleground. Eric alternated between total withdrawal or unreasonable demand; many nights he turned his back to Ellen and went right off to sleep, while other times, especially when she was especially exhausted from a rough day, he would be insistent almost to the point of abusiveness.

During the ensuing months, their marital and familial life reached a nadir and Ellen many times wondered how much more she could stand of this belligerent, pejorative self-destructing man Eric had become. But she loved him and they had a lifetime of shared memories and pleasures. She knew his faults but she also appreciated the special satisfaction that comes from living with a person whose attitudes and tastes were similar since they were developed jointly during their many years together. Ellen had been meeting many men of Eric's age in her new career, and to her, they all suffered by comparison to Eric. She realized that there was no other man for her, and whatever had to be done and lived through to get him back to himself was worth doing.

Eventually Eric found a business that was ideal for him and their life began to improve as he became happier and more fulfilled.

Reverse Penis Envy

Eric and Peter went through a crisis for which nothing and no one had prepared them. Although their fathers and their fathers before them may have gone through mid-life crises of readjusting self-images and goals, their difficulties were never compounded by the added complication of having to face a suddenly successful wife just as you have to face up to your own limitations. The sudden role reversal can be shattering: "Where is that rock I married?" says she. "Where is that supportive wife I married?" says he. "What happened to dependable Dad? Who is this ogre who's making all of us miserable? Why is he mistreating our mother when she works so hard now?" say the children.

His feelings are in absolute chaos as he subconsciously wishes he were she. "She's off and running and I'm stalled and stale. She's going through the excitement of self-discovery and finding facets of ability she never knew she had and I'm finding areas of inability I never knew I had." He sees his diminished image reflected in her attitudes of antagonism and lessening respect and it eats away at him. These corrosive elements are bound to show up in the bedroom, which becomes the sole arena where he can exert absolute power. A woman cannot have sex at will, she must depend on the will of the man. The old stereotype of the sex-resistant wife with chronic headache excuses has made men feel comfortable and not threatened by a spouse who displays disinterest in sex. But a woman who is classically in the compliant position of awaiting the man's readiness for sex can feel devastated by the rebuff of a husband who ignores her night after night. If she outdoes him during the day, thereby making him feel like less of a man, what better way to punish her than make her feel like less of a woman at night?

If the dreadful dynamics of this situation are allowed to continue unchecked, it could lead to the destruction of the marriage. As in any dispute, both husband and wife see themselves as the injured party. Each one bears a terrible burden, but hers is more apparent and she tends to get more sympathy from friends and family. She not only goes to work and carries the full financial load, but also must run the home, soothe the fears and angers of the frightened children, and then deal with the tantrums and erratic behavior of her husband. To her, the present is intolerable and the future seems hopeless. His position, however, is even rougher because he sees all these public signs of disgust and disapproval which only confirm his rapidly growing loss of self-respect and he just sinks further and further into a morass of self-pity and self-loathing that can lead to total paralysis of activity.

Under these circumstances, outside counselling is almost always necessary. It is vital that both husband and wife learn to understand the forces at work in the situation so that they and the family can live through it. When it's over, things will never be the same. Perceptions of each other will now be different as a result of the weaknesses and strengths never before exposed.

As I mentioned in an earlier chapter, many of the people I interviewed mentioned being "taken care of" as a prime motivation for marrying. At this point in the marriage, both partners' concepts of who needs to take care of whom and how will change. Ellen has learned that she can support herself and is not as dependent on Eric as she had thought all these years. She now enjoys a sense of self-worth that makes her a stronger and happier person. She no longer has the fears about her financial future which are harbored by every wife who has based her entire married life on the earning ability of her husband. Eric in turn has a new respect for his wife, a feeling he can enjoy once his banes of self-doubt and self-pity have been conquered. He is truly proud of Ellen and now regards her as a peer in areas he never considered her even minimally competent. This rearrangement of evaluations has given both people a new sense of priorities as to what each wants and needs from marriage NOW. There's the operational word—now. People change the times and the times change people, and adaptation is the key to survival.

Follow the New Leader

"She spent the first half of our married life following me, now I'll be perfectly happy spending the second half following her." The first time I heard those words they came from a middle-aged man from Georgia, and I thought, "How great. Maybe times are starting to change." Then as I went along interviewing couples throughout the country, I heard the same statement from men whose wives had embarked on new midlife careers and I began to realize that times are not starting to change—they have already changed.

Over and over, I ran into couples who had followed a procedure that would never have occurred twenty years ago: They discussed and made plans for, as they consistently put it, the next stage of their marriage, which involved the wife's after-parenting role.

Years ago, it was assumed that the wife, whose children were grown and had become less dependent, would spend more of her time shopping, lunching with friends and in charitable activities. But now both she and her husband realize that she is capable of more and is entitled to an individual life instead of one that is totally derived from the family. This new consciousness must be attributed to the women's movement.

What seems to have happened is that the men not only see it as right and just for their wives to embark upon careers of their own, but as a symbol of their own open mindedness and modern intelligence. Where years ago the fact that his wife worked was a badge of male shame and a public admission that he could not support his family, today it is a source of pride.

I recently sat in on a business meeting of a large company with three male executives in their thirties and forties as two of them were discussing their wives' careers and how they worked out the household details. The third man sat silently. When I asked him what his wife did, he seemed somewhat embarrassed to admit that she just stayed home with the children.

With this new equality in roles in marriage, it is inevitable that times should occur when one partner has to be more equal than the other. Like when his new job means moving to another city and she is forced to give up her job and move with him. That used to be the norm. But not any more. In almost all cases where the wives were either working or preparing for new careers, the husbands stated that they would be perfectly willing to relocate to suit the needs of their wives' careers. This was consistent from men in Georgia, Idaho, Indiana—all over the United States, not just in the so-called sophisticated urban centers.

Sometimes the adjustments and adaptations they are willing to make are astounding.

* * *

Paul and Norma had lived on a small farm in Iowa since they were married eighteen years before. The maintenance was handled by hired help and the farm was not regarded as the family's source of livelihood. Paul was an executive with a major company in the area. The evening they learned that the eldest of their two children was accepted in the college of his choice, Norma and Paul had the kind of important discussion they had whenever a milestone was reached in the family.

"Now what do I do with the next part of my life?" Norma asked.

Organization and planning was Paul's strong point in business and he tended to carry over the same approach to handling his family responsibilities.

"I think it's time we made a seven-year plan," he said. "Where do we want to be in seven years and how do we want to go about getting there?"

Usually Norma kidded Paul about his introduction of efficiency techniques to their home life, but this time it seemed appropriate.

"Now that Paul Jr. will be off to college in the Fall, and Tommy has just another year of high school, I'd better prepare to do something with myself. But what can I do?"

Paul thought for a moment. "How about counseling—the kind of thing we do in church? You're very good at it." They belonged to an unusually large church in the area and were both very involved in community-help activities. "Why don't you check out the university for a major in that area?"

Norma conferred with the admissions office and found that she had the prerequisites for a specific major in community counseling and psychology, so she matriculated and became a full-time student at the same time that her son entered college in another city. After about six months into her major, she found she really hated the subject, but was especially enthralled with learning German, which was required for the major since so much of the literature was in that language. She also found that she was enjoying and was very good at economics. After conferring with her guidance counselor and Paul, she switched her major to finance with a minor in German. By her second year, she had a 3.9 grade point average and knew exactly what sort of career she would head for upon graduation.

Just at that time, Paul was offered an excellent position as vice-president of a good company in Milwaukee. The opportunity and money was extraordinary and he could not turn the job down. Not for a moment did they consider Norma quitting college and following him. Her education was deemed of equal importance to Paul's career, so they made a decision that would have been unthinkable twenty years ago. Paul took a small apartment in Milwaukee, Norma stayed in Iowa, and he flew home every weekend.

When I asked him how this worked into their seven-year plan, he said: "When she gets out in two years, the way it looks is that she'll have a number of great job offers in international finance . . . she's already had some nibbles. Wherever her job takes her, that's where we'll go. She followed me around for the first part of our married life—there were years when we had to sublease the farm and move to another city that my company sent me to. Now it's my turn to follow her."

When I brought up the subject of jealousy—wouldn't he be just the tiniest bit envious of the new hot-shot executive that his wife might become—he answered with a big smile:

"Hell, no. It makes me the smart guy. Because I had the brains to pick a winner, didn't I?"

You could foretell the continuing success of this marriage because both partners were willing to accept change with equanimity. The basis of their relationship was love and respect, and whatever direction they were drawn into by life occurrence, they would handle it with consideration for each other and the implicit acceptance that both individuals were of equal importance.

Sometimes couples try to follow this path to parity but outside forces such as family conspire against their attempts.

* * *

Jim and Sybil considered themselves very happily married. They had gone through some Entry Level trauma when Sybil refused to move to another city where Jim's company had sent him because she was in the middle of finishing up her master's degree in education in a local college and could not successfully transfer without losing credits. So for one year, they lived apart and spent only weekends together. It was rough for a newly married couple trying to adjust to the pulls of married life, and it was made rougher by the constant harangues and dire warnings from Jim's mother about how Sybil risked danger daily by allowing her husband to dwell alone in a strange city which was crawling with single predatory females. What kind of a wife would send her husband off to be untended and uncared for? Who would make him hot dinners?

They survived the year in spite of everything, and Sybil moved to Jim's city after her graduation and found an excellent job in the school system. Two children came along and Sybil managed with part-time help and daycare until they were old enough to be in school all day with hours that coincided with hers.

During the years, Jim had been offered a promotion within the company, but the job would have entailed moving back to the city they had left behind, and Sybil refused to give up her position and be forced to start all over again elsewhere. Now, fifteen years later, Jim's company once again offered him a promotion, but this was a major step up within the organization that would put him in line for the top corporate level. This time it was an offer he could not refuse without sealing himself into junior executive status forever. He knew that his future was riding on his answer.

Sybil was alternately furious and depressed with the prospect of moving away. She had just been made supervisor of her department, taught a course at night in the local college, and was on the boards of numerous professional and local organizations. She had made a very successful place for herself in the community and was highly regarded. Now Jim was asking her to give up her years of work for his future. They agonized over the decision and were close to coming to a reasonable solution for both of them when Jim made the error of mentioning it to his mother.

"What kind of wife doesn't help her husband get ahead? A schoolteacher you can be anywhere—but the head of a corporation chance comes once in a lifetime. What kind of selfish wife do you have? It's outrageous. In my day there would have been no question."

Jim knew enough to avoid mentioning his mother's comments to Sybil, but he had reckoned without his mother's ability to handle communications directly. She immediately phoned Sybil to convey her opinions. Sybil was infuriated by her mother-in-law's allegations that Sybil's work was minor league and that her achievements were of minimal importance and easily transportable.

"For the few dollars you get for teaching college they'll be glad to take you anywhere—there are plenty of those kind of colleges where you'll be going. And high school teachers they're crying for everywhere—you won't have any trouble."

In a few well-chosen words, she managed to reduce Sybil's entire career to meaningless busywork. After that conversation, Sybil announced that she refused to move and if Jim wanted the job, he'd have to choose between her and it. For two days afterwards, Jim was unable to bring up the subject without Sybil storming out of the room with some allusion to his moving in with his mother as the solution to the problem.

Finally, one evening when they were in bed, he broached it again.

"Look, Syb, I know how you've worked to get where you are and I think it's terrific. And you know how I've worked to get where I am. But let's look at it this way. If I don't move now, I'm doomed to never go higher. You know that a promotion turndown marks you as unambitious, unmotivated and unqualified for advancement ever. I turned down the promotion fifteen years ago. If I do it again, that finishes me. I'll always be just where I am today and that terrifies me. I know it's unfair to ask you to give up all you've built here. But there are a lot of schools where we'll be going, but only one major company like mine anywhere. The fact is you have options that I don't. And on that basis alone, I'm asking you to make this move."

Sybil thought about it for just a few moments and then said.

"O.K. we'll move, but on one condition."

"Name it," Jim said eagerly.

"That you tell your mother the only reason I agreed to go was that you promised to buy me a two-karat diamond ring. That kind of bargaining she understands and she'll respect me like crazy." She smiled. "I don't want her to think I settle cheap."

"And What Do You Do?"

When I taught a course called "How to Start Your Own Business" in the Women's Studies department of the University of Connecticut, my classes were filled with women who sought a mid-life change and thought entrepreneurism was the route to take. A number of them were really unwilling victims of the women's movement who were being embarrassed by the "And what do *you* do?" question at dinner parties and the scornful reaction when they answered, "I'm a housewife."

It's a shame that the women's movement was so misunderstood by some women who saw it as an enforced drive to send them out of the home instead of what it really is—a vehicle of choice. What it has achieved is to offer women options they could never consider before which allow them to stay at home if they wish or pursue a career if they prefer, with no stigma attached to either route.

Many of my students had serious intentions of starting a business but were completely unfamiliar with procedures and demands of the business world, sometimes to the point of total unreality. There were two women who announced they planned to open a coffee bean store and wanted to know, during the very first session, how they would go about franchising. When they showed up at the second session, they informed us that they would be unable to attend the following two classes since they were going to South America on a buying trip. "It's deductible, you know," they said airily. "From what?" I asked. "You don't even have a store yet." But they didn't care because this entire adventure was being subsidized by their indulgent husbands.

And there lies the crux of the problem of many couples' way of dealing with the wife's mid-life desire for change. One woman told me that when her children were all in school, she told her husband that she had to "find herself" (you'll pardon the expression, but it's a direct quote). She concluded her announcement with the demand that he give her $25,000 to start a business because if he didn't, she would only cost him that much in psychiatric fees.

Starting a business is the route many re-entry women take who do not wish to go for long schooling and are unqualified for any specific job in the marketplace. The Small Business Administration's statistics indicate that women constitute one of the largest start-up entrepreneur groups of the past few years. They are not always aware of the full ramifications of opening a store and many embark upon retail enterprises without realizing that being a storekeeper is not just a series of pleasant social interchanges with customers who drop in. Rather, it entails financial responsibilities as well as many pressing obligations, such as being there six days a week, which means no pleasant Saturdays on the tennis court or golf course when everyone else is there having a great time. That's why every neighborhood has its share of boutiques and gourmet food shops that are opened usually by two women and often closed within six months. However, thousands of women have started businesses and done superbly, sometimes changing the path of their marriages as a result.

When I lectured to the National Needlepoint Association a few years ago, a group consisting of thousands of owners of needlepoint shops, my audience was predominantly women who had started and built successful businesses. What was interesting was the large percentage of husbands who had joined their wives in what eventually became the family enterprise. In almost all cases, the husband had indulged the "little woman" by subsidizing her in starting what he fully expected would be a dismal failure. As the business prospered, he began to take an interest and come in on Saturdays. Before long, if he was a career employee, he would become enamored of the prospect of being his own boss and eventually quit his job to work full time with his wife. This inevitably brought about a dramatic change in their relationship, since he was really now working for her. But if a good marriage existed before this new role-switch, it worked out well, as he began to take over certain areas of running the business which she preferred not to do, while she could concentrate on the creative aspects that she enjoyed.

The Wondrous Ways of Love

The interaction of her rebirth and his reconciliation often turns up surprising revelations in a marriage. Like all activities that occur during the years of a long relationship, people just perform them and rarely take the time to evaluate feelings and to understand changes that have taken place.

A perfect example of this came from a woman I interviewed who started out by saying what almost everyone opened with:

"Why, sure, I'd love to be interviewed. But I must tell you that mine is not a typical marriage."

As though there is such a thing as a typical marriage. But everyone likes to believe that he or she is somewhat different and in ways unique. After all, who likes to admit to being average?

* * *

She married a man who was a career Army man twenty-seven years ago. He had rigid ideas of the male marital role and she, being inexperienced and the product of a conventional Italian Catholic home, accepted his behavior as she believed a good wife must.

During all the early years of her marriage, she deeply resented the fact that he went out with his friends a few nights a week and left her with the two babies. And when she wanted to take an evening off, she had to ask him if he would do her the favor of baby-sitting . . . with his own children! Most of their homes were on Army posts, so her husband never saw any other kind of marital relationship than the dominant male and the waiting-at-home wife. She hated the life, but never felt she had the right to voice her opinions, because how would that change things? This was his career, and when she married him, this was what she had to expect.

But when her daughers were in high school, she decided she could now make some life for herself away from the Army, and she applied for a job in a local chain of supermarkets.

"I had absolutely no skills," she said, "but they ran an ad in the paper offering a long list of jobs and I felt that I was smart and ought to be able to fit in somewhere."

After taking an aptitude test to see where they could place her, she was called back and told she had scored exceptionally high. In their opinion, she would make an excellent executive *secretary*. (These were the pre-women's-movement days when that was how they slotted capable females.) Since she could not type or take shorthand, they sent her to school for training and she shortly became the secretary to one of the company vice-presidents. Her husband was surprised at her wanting to work at all, but looked upon the episode as unimportant and unthreatening. After all, she was only a secretary, a perfectly respectable woman's job. But she was very smart, and soon tired of the work and found another job as an executive secretary for the sales manager of a computer reselling company in the area. The work interested her and she had a real talent for it plus an exceptional ability to handle people. Soon she was doing much of her boss's work and having a wonderful time. When he left for another job, the company offered her the position he had just vacated—and now, suddenly, she was the sales manager of a sizable company.

Just about this time, her husband's twenty-year-stint in the service was over. He retired with a pension, and found himself a job with a local shipping company doing work similar to that which he had performed for the Army.

"We had absolutely nothing to talk about now," she said. "He was totally disinterested in my job and I sure didn't find his work fascinating. I joined a local little theater group and had a great time, but he hated to come to the cast parties; he really felt uncomfortable with my friends."

"What do you do together at all?" I asked.

"Go out to dinner," she answered.

"What do you talk about all evening?"

"The kids," she answered.

In the meantime, she was traveling around the country to seminars and conventions, and was highly regarded by the entire industry.

I listened to her story and then asked: "Tell me, why do you stay with this man?" She thought for a moment and said, "I don't know."

Later on, we had dinner together and I talked about my marriage. "I'm lucky, I guess. I have the kind of husband who thinks I'm the greatest, smartest and most gorgeous woman in the universe and tells me that every day."

She looked at me strangely. "My husband is that way, too," she said. I was stunned. Somehow I had envisioned her husband as taciturn and not given to compliments or words of love.

"Whenever we walk into a roomful of people, he turns to me and says 'Hon, you're the best-looking woman in the room.' And when I gain weight, which I always do because I'm one of those yo-yo dieters, and I look in the mirror in my old baggy sweatshirt and pants that I wear when I put on a few pounds and complain about how fat I've gotten, he always says, 'You're nuts. You have a great body.' "

She and I looked at each other silently for a few moments as the full import of what she was saying reached her.

"Now do you know why you stay with him?" I asked.

He adored and admired her, and that total endorsement gave her the power and belief in herself to go out and conquer the world. She was a nice-looking but not stunning woman, but she would always see herself in his loving eyes and that made her feel wonderful.

I have seen beautiful women who are married to men who constantly criticize their appearance so that they eventually end up carrying themselves like unattractive women because they are riddled with insecurity. This woman comported herself like a queen because that's what her husband made her feel like. And for that she loved him and needed him and was perfectly willing to cope with the other drawbacks in her marriage.

Marriage is the least static of all institutions and the most malleable. If the relationship is based on love, trust and caring, it can be twisted and reshaped and not only retain its value but actually become strengthened from the restructuring. As one man said to me: "If you love each other, you should never give up. You go through it and stick it out because that's when the good stuff comes."

THE SIXTH LEVEL

Hum-Drum

The most general survey shows us that the two foes of human happiness are pain and boredom.

—ARTHUR SCHOPENHAUER

The Bane of Boredom

Living together for twenty to thirty years brings bonding but also boredom. During the first five Levels, you were occupied with adapting to each other, working to build a financial future, and having a family. Just dealing with the difficulties of daily living kept you challenged and busy. Now comes the calm. The kids are away in college, or off somewhere, and the homefront has quieted down. Husband and wife are established in their careers and life has settled into a satisfactory and uneventful routine.

Now the big problem is you have no big problems. So in order to make life interesting, you have to create a few. Since reality is pretty much taken care of, it's time to deal in the abstract, which leads to bouts of questioning the Meaning of Life: "Why am I here?" and "Is this all there is?" Compounding the confusion is that your friends seem to be dropping dead all over the place, or having major health disasters, and you have become horribly aware of your own mortality. The tendency is to recall all the things you wanted to do but never did, and maybe some things you never even dreamed of, and to get desperate to do them all now before your precious time is up. Since skydiving and climbing the Himalayas is somewhat impractical, the easiest route in this rebellion against age is to have an affair.

* * *

Donna was 52 and had been happily married to Jeff for 27 years. Their children were in college and Donna had worked in the family hardware store for the past fifteen years. She always enjoyed the activity of handling the inventory, dealing with customers and all the busy details involved in running a large retail establishment. But now she was becoming restless, and oftentimes downright cranky. After one evening when the teenage ticket-taker at the movie theatre asked if Donna and Jeff wanted senior citizen discounts, she became impossibly irritable for days. Jeff noticed the change and was lovingly concerned.

"What's wrong, honey? Are you feeling O.K.?" She couldn't explain her malaise, only that she felt tired and empty most of the time.

"What you need is a vacation," said Jeff. "Why don't you run up and spend a few days with Marge?" Marge was a childhood friend who, when widowed two years before, had moved to a small town in the mountains and begun a career of creating and selling ceramics and crafts. Donna felt a bit guilty and strange, since she had never gone anywhere without Jeff during their entire marriage, but with his encouragement, she went.

The few days stretched into a week as Donna began to enjoy a life of total freedom from responsibility. Especially when she met Marge's current boyfriend's friend Lyle, a local builder who had been divorced three times and now began coming on to Donna. She felt flattered, desirable, young . . . emotions that had not been aroused in her for years. Vulnerable and under the most conducive circumstances, she succumbed to a sexual relationship. Upon her returning home, she told Jeff that she "needed space" (one of the most unfortunate and overused expressions of the day) and left a puzzled and anxious husband to move back to the mountain town in a small apartment near Marge.

She began an affair with Lyle that lasted two months, which was his usual span of interest. During this period, Donna returned home from time to time to explain to Jeff how she was a free spirit and he was a conventional being who could never "communicate," and maybe they should separate for a while. Jeff was very hurt and unhappy, and found it embarrassing to explain her absence to his customers. But he loved her deeply and felt their marriage was too important and solid to destroy, and refused to give her up. When Lyle dumped her, Donna was devastated and started to spend a good deal of her days and evenings with Marge, whose life always appeared idyllic to her. Soon the freedom began to pall as loneliness set in, and she began to miss the pleasant companionable evenings with her husband, and the unexciting but satisfying details of running their home with the kids calling and dropping in. and the wonderful secure feeling of living with someone who loved her unreservedly and thought she looked beautiful even when she'd put on five pounds.

So she went home, and they, literally, lived happily ever after.

Ria D. Simon, the well-known Stamford, Connecticut, matrimonial lawyer, tells me that a good number of her cases involve women in the forties and fifties who claim they need "space" and "communication," and break up their marriages in pursuit of these elusive goals. The Hum-Drum Level is a danger point for marriage today because the women's movement encourages women to be independent, which many wives misinterpret to mean irresponsible. They think it gives them license to take off at will in search of so-called self-expression. Ennui with a marriage of long standing is not new with this generation; what is new is our flagrantly overt way of handling it. Thirty years ago or three hundred years ago a wife like Donna might have relieved her restlessness with extra-marital activity, but with discretion. If her dalliance were discovered, societal scorn could drive her to an Anna Karenina fate; there was never an accepted justification for female adultery. Today the word "cuckold" has been virtually dropped from the language and a husband whose wife has strayed doesn't beat her, he understands her. Certainly discussion is better than stoning her to death in the village square. But freedom from retribution does not bring freedom from responsibility and going off to have a wild fling is not independent self-expression but merely selfish self-indulgence that will inflict pain on those you love. Of course men have been doing this for centuries on the assumption that rank has its privileges. Today's heightened consciousness about sex discrimination frees women to behave as men. But do we really want to adopt the privileges that are rank?

A marriage that has come through twenty to thirty years has too much invested in it to be destroyed by an innocuous discontent. There are other steps that can be taken to relieve the situation, changes in lifestyle that a couple can effect together or even separately without inflicting irreparable damage on the relationship. The blahs that come at this stage of marriage are the kind of letdown one feels upon winning a hard-fought victory for a cause. After the exhilaration and camaraderie of battle are over, the quiet can be unsettling. So what do you do, destroy the prize you fought for just to create new excitement—or learn ways to enjoy the new tranquility?

Macho & Mortality

Men carry some heavy baggage through life—the fear of minifying masculinity. When a man of twenty fails to have an erection, he sees it as temporary mortification. But when a man of fifty finds that his libido can't raise his penis, he sees this as a portent of the future. Add the fact that three of his friends had heart bypasses last month, and all his new business associates are calling him "sir," and you have a man who is ready for "me-ism." To cap off his sense of diminishing life force, he comes home at night to smartass kids who no longer regard him as big daddy and a self-actualized wife for whom he is no longer the kingpin. It is inevitable that he turns to narcissism and the pursuit of fitness and fantasy.

* * *

All his friends saw it. Martin was suffering from the Peter Pan syndrome—he wanted to be young forever. He took up jogging ferociously, joined a health club and worked out three times a week. His gray hair became suspiciously darker by the day and was now being combed across the top of his head to cover the bald spot. When the attractive 35-year-old woman who had just joined his corporate department turned to him for daily advice, he was pleased. And when she asked if they could have dinner together one evening a week—Dutch, of course—so that he could help her to adapt faster to the needs of the company of which he was controller, he was flattered. When he told his wife, Penny, that he would be having dinner in town on Tuesdays with a colleague, he failed to mention that the colleague was a beautiful recently-divorced woman and that their business discussions were supplemented with personal confidences. Penny was happy to see the change in Martin; there was a spring in his step that she hadn't seen for months, and their sex life went from desultory to exciting, especially Tuesday nights when he seemed to initiate all sorts of previously untried erotica like fellatio and cunnilingus. Up to this point, Martin's business dinners were all talk and no action. And then a friend told Penny that she had seen Martin and a beautiful redhead dining together.

"You lied to me! I trusted you and you're having a dirty affair, you lying son-of-a-bitch!" screamed Penny when Martin walked in the door that evening. She had spent the day planning how she would confront him with her knowledge and had evolved a cleverly worded accusation to be presented with calm nobility. But all the emotions of hurt and betrayal erupted the moment she saw her husband,

and she spewed forth a diatribe that horrified her children and her. Martin was stunned and shamed but insisted that the meetings were harmless and platonic. Which they were up to that point. But if this were true, why did he feel the need to dissemble, Penny asked rightfully. And those Tuesday night sex performances, wasn't that just practicing on his wife techniques he had just learned from his lover? In reality his horniness came not from his own erotic adventures, but from listening to details of the sexual difficulties the young colleague had with her divorced husband. But who would believe that?

Their home life became a shambles. Penny could not control her anger. If Martin arrived home five minutes late any evening, she accused him of having been with his "woman." The children were miserable and detested being brought into the battle between their parents, with their sympathies being pulled both ways. The couple's social life came to a virtual standstill as friends demurred at being made spectators to Penny's vitriolic outbursts. The sad truth was that Martin loved his wife and, though flattered by the attentions of a young attractive woman at a time when he felt his appeal waning, he had no real wish to jeopardize his marriage. But his home life was becoming untenable and the sympathetic ear of his Tuesday dinner companion was more and more important.

Since their needs dovetailed—her husband's rejection and his wife's repulsion evoked a common wish for love and attention—the relationship became a self-fulfilling prophesy.

Martin should have been happy. His male friends treated him with smirking "you dog you" envy as he lived every middle-aged man's fantasy, but he felt a pervasive heaviness and misery. He dreaded coming home to the cold implacable person Penny had become and longed for the happy warmth of their old life but did not know how to revive it. Penny became angrier and more punitive which drove him to spend more time with his lover whom he did not love, making Penny even angrier. During all this time, though Penny and Martin had shrieking fights during which the word "divorce" was mentioned, neither one took any steps to dissolve their marriage because, through it all, they loved each other and wanted to stay together. Except they had now gotten themselves into a bind that neither one knew how to break and the strain on both of them was tremendous. Then late one afternoon, Penny received a phone call advising her that Martin had suffered a heart attack at his desk and was in the intensive care unit of a downtown hospital.

Penny spent the next week at the hospital at her husband's side. He was permitted visitors at scheduled times, but the only persons he wanted to see were his wife and children. His lover came once and Martin asked her not to return; in his mind, she was to blame for his condition as her aggressive seduction had caused the stress that brought on the attack. He discussed this with Penny and they happily agreed on their common enemy. The choice of a convenient scapegoat enabled them to fix blame elsewhere and allow them to both feel fault-free. Martin recovered totally and they resumed their life together.

The problem ended happily but the catalyst for the solution was a near tragedy. It should not have come to that. Admittedly a mate's infidelity is tough to take under any circumstances. The pains of hurt and betrayal are palpable and violent reaction is instinctual. But reason and logic must play a part. The marriage vow is for better or for worse; this is clearly part of the worse. Penny and Martin had been happily married for twenty-five years and truly loved each other. Martin's sudden clutching at youth should have alerted Penny to the fears that were troubling him. For her this was a signal to be especially aware and sympathetic.

Unfortunately in the view of our society, unlike the Asian, age does not bring wisdom but uselessness. Thus the first signs of age are enough to drive a vital man into panic as he sees the portent of a powerless future. It is the loss of his power and powers that he fears. Professionally he will be supplanted with younger people who will regard his advice as antedeluvian. He may be seeing that response now to a degree as they talk with a computer literacy that leaves him behind. Then he comes home and his children, who used to turn to him for advice and guidance, now scorn his values and question his value. He's not such a hotshot in the bedroom anymore as sex with the same partner has lost its lustre.

Martin was a forceful person with a strong ego. That's the kind who has the toughest time accepting diminishment of demand. Penny should have recognized that and realized the reason for his Tuesday evening meetings as soon as she heard about it. She might have handled it any number of ways. One method would have been to kid him into abashed admission: "Why didn't you tell me your colleague is a gorgeous redhead? I wouldn't mind. I have lunch with men in my job all the time—I think it's fun. What do you talk about?"

With that approach, Martin would still feel flattered by the younger woman's interest but the dangerous clandestine quality would be eliminated. As a matter of fact, Martin admitted that many times his colleague told him interesting things that he longed to discuss with Penny but desisted because he feared her reaction. He regarded Penny as his best and most intimate friend, as she viewed him. Whenever either heard anything interesting, the instinctive reaction was to go home and talk about it. If Penny had treated the whole matter casually and openly, it would have gone no further. In fact, she could have used it to fuel Martin's faltering ego by joking to friends while he beamed proudly, "What do you think of my dashing Lothario here? He has a stunning young redhead in his office who thinks he's a cross between Burt Reynolds and Henry Kissinger!"

The Hum-Drum Level is a watershed in marriage. It is a time that imposes heavy strains on the relationship because it comes at a crucial personal changing point for the partners. It is a juncture for questioning and it is important that they give each other the right answers. If the erratic behavior of a spouse upsets the other, precipitous emotional reaction, natural as it may be, can create serious damage and persistence may push them into a result that neither one wants. Like divorce. It behooves the injured party, before embarking upon a course of reactive behavior, to think it through with these important three words in mind: "To what end?"

Do you want to drive them away or bring them back? If a husband or wife has suddenly found another arena more attractive, why confirm that temporary error in judgment by converting the home into an unwelcoming wasteland of invective and haranguing? Granted it takes an iron control to act normally or lovingly to a spouse you feel has wronged you. But if you regard it as a temporary illness, an of-the-moment aberration that is a sign of inadequacy and self-doubt and not a rejection of all you hold dear, you can deal with it logically and effectively. If you both truly love each other and have a lifetime of caring and respect to bank on—and you know that your spouse really wants the marriage to last, then don't let your ego stand in the way of a sensible handling of the situation.

Cosmetic Surgery: The Remake Route

"I was feeling low so I got a lift," the 48-year-old woman told me. The peaceful, secure and relatively untroubled existence she and her husband had struggled to achieve had become dull, the future held no thrilling surprises and she longed for a change. So she had a face lift and it gave her just the impetus needed to pull herself out of the kind of doldrums that can wreak havoc in a marriage.

"When a married woman comes to me and wants a total remake—face, breasts, stomach—I know the surgery is just a metaphor for a deeper problem and I spend time questioning the patient's motives," says Dr. Norman J. Pastorek, the New York cosmetic surgeon. He will point out that cosmetic surgery may not be the panacea for a troubled marriage and will caution the patient against placing too high expectations on the outcome. "But if comparatively minor procedures like removing bags and lines from the eyes or fat from under the chin make her happier with herself, it's worth doing." A woman is taught from childhood that her success will always be tied up with her looks. At this Hum-Drum

Level in her marriage when the zest seems to have disappeared, the signs of the onset of aging presaging the dimunition of attractiveness and sex appeal can have a damaging effect on her and her marital relationship. If plastic surgery can give her a sense of renewal and improved self-esteem, that's great.

Of course, men, too, although they will rarely acknowledge it, are turning to cosmetic surgery at this time of their lives for similar reasons. Since vanity is usually regarded as unmanly, most males who get facial redos in their fifties and sixties attribute their action to the youth demands of the marketplace. "I got tired of being treated with deference in the office," one 58-year-old man told me. But another admitted, "I just didn't like what I saw in the mirror every morning."

Dr. Pastorek also pointed out the need for the individual who is planning surgery to clarify the reasons to his or her spouse. "A husband or wife whose partner wants to undergo cosmetic surgery tends to wonder why. 'What does she really have in mind? Is she having an affair or planning to?' 'Is he going on the hunt for younger women?' 'Is he tired of me?' It is vital for the well-being of the marriage that the prospective patient explain to his or her partner that she's doing it for herself, to make her feel better and happier." The doctor mentioned the conflicts he has seen occur in his office when the wife turns to her husband and says "Well, what do you think . . . should I have the face lift?"

"The husband is put into an untenable position. If he says, 'No,' she'll feel he is denying her need and is not being supportive. If he says, 'Yes,' she feels rejected and unlovely: "So he really thinks I look like an old bag.' It's a no-win situation."

Restlessness, dissatisfaction with the status quo,

desire for change . . . these are the motives that move women and men to take minor and sometimes major steps in their lives at this time of life. Altering your appearance is one way; changing your lifestyle is another.

The Gauguin Syndrome

"Let's give up the rat-race and sail off to Tahiti," says the humdrummed-out husband as the couple sit on a Carribean beach and contemplate the return Monday to a predictable existence. "Or maybe we should buy a little hotel here on this island. Wouldn't that be a great new life?"

"Sure," she thinks to herself. "I'll be in the kitchen or making beds while Mr. Congeniality here will be tending bar and chatting with the guests."

The desire to escape from the mundane, to be adventurous and effect big changes in lifestyle, can become pressing issues to someone who would like to feel that his best years could be ahead of him instead of behind. The usual reaction of the disaffected is to opt for radical overall change rather than taking the sensible route of pinpointing the reasons for discontent and merely correcting them.

One woman I spoke to was driving her husband crazy with the demand that they leave their New York City home of twenty-five years which she now regarded as four steps below Sodom and Gommorah, and move to the only-place-in-the-world-for-her, San Diego. Since that would entail his commuting weekly to his job in New York, the proposal was rather unrealistic. Eventually the problem was happily resolved when she discovered that a lovely suburb of New York offered the same clean, slower-paced qualities she sought on the other side of the country.

Many men and women have found that career changes at this point in their lives bring them the new lease on life they sought.

* * *

Mark had been in the retail business all his working life. It was not the career of his choice but rather of expediency since his father had built a sizable chain store enterprise which offered a tempting executive job and salary upon Mark's graduation from college.

He really loved the world and pace of academia and wanted to teach at the university level, but the requirement for a few more years of studying for advanced degrees was disparaged by his father. "Invest all that time and money for more school so that you end up making a lousy thirty or forty thousand dollars a year? You can make fifty thousand here right now." The terms were too seductive and his will not strong enough for Mark to fight his father, so he went into the business and regretted it forever.

He married Rita, his college girlfriend, they had three children, two cars, a large comfortable home in the suburbs and a reasonably good and happy life. Then a short time after their big twenty-fifth anniversary party, Rita began to notice a change in Mark, a discontent and irritability and a totally depressed withdrawal every Sunday evening. An astute and sensitive woman, Rita knew enough to wait for the moment when Mark would be ready to reveal the source of his problem. One day he came home with the catalog from a local college and he seemed more alive than he had been in weeks.

"Look at the curriculum they offer in marketing and retailing," he said excitedly.

Rita was puzzled. "Why would you want to take those courses? You could teach that stuff."

Mark smiled. "Exactly."

Then Rita knew what had been bothering him. He began to pour out to her how much he hated going to work which made Sunday evenings miserable since they were the lead-ins to Monday. How weary he was of the sameness of the details and difficulties he had to deal with daily.

"We have enough money to pay for the kids' college, and to live fairly comfortably if we cut back a bit on the luxuries here and there. What I really want to do is teach. Why can't I do it now?"

They talked way into the night and his enthusiasm sparked Rita's support and encouragement. She had helped him in the stores and would now go out and get a job. There would be some money coming from the liquidation of the business—it had deteriorated into a non-salable condition due to a combination of factors like dying downtown locations and Mark's diminishing interest. That plus Rita's salary and their savings could certainly keep them going, maybe not in the same grand country club lifestyle, but who really needed that stuff anyway?

Mark approached the college and others in the area and was taken on to teach a few courses. They sold their house and traded down for a smaller one using the profit to create earnings, Rita got a position in the buying office of a large retail operation in the area, Mark began to do the marketing and cooking since he was home more and he became a dedicated gourmet cook, and they were ecstatically happy. There was a shifting of roles in their relationship that brought new zest and elan to both them and their marriage. Lying in bed one night after a particularly satisfactory session of lovemaking, Mark turned to Rita and said, "Isn't it great? Now we have a whole new twenty-five years to look forward to."

THE SEVENTH LEVEL

Freedom

Freedom is nothing else but a chance to be better.

—Albert Camus

Freedom, It's Wonderful

Lucy hung up the phone after a conversation with her daughter and sighed. Her husband, John, who was sitting nearby reading the newspaper asked sharply: "What's the matter? Something wrong with Marcia or the kids?" "Nope," said Lucy sadly. "But you'll see for yourself. They're all coming here this weekend." John closed the paper. "What the hell do you mean they're coming this weekend? Didn't you tell them we had plans to go to the lake?" Lucy looked depressed. "Sure I told her. But she said that Andy will be away on a business trip and she hates to be alone in the house, and couldn't we go to the lake next weekend. What could I do?"

John threw the paper down angrily. "Son-of-a-bitch—won't we ever be free of those kids of ours? We've given them half our lives. Now it's time for US."

* * *

John and Lucy had been married for thirty-five years. During that time, John had built a small manufacturing business that had grown into a highly lucrative enterprise. They had two sons and two daughters all of whom had gone through college and graduate schools and were now successful professionals. Lucy had followed the traditional route of full-time mother and housewife until the last child entered high school, at which time she had resumed her career and had worked her way up to the position of executive director of a local social service organization. Three years ago, after the wedding of their second daughter, which was held in their home, Lucy and John sat in the now retidied living room and Lucy said: "Do you realize this was the last of it? This was the last child-expenditure we'll ever have? Of course, we may have to help them out here and there, but that's different." John smiled broadly. "Right. Now we can spend all the money on us. How about that Greek Island cruise we've been talking about for ten years?"

After they came home from the trip, a new type of relationship began to evolve between them as they started to develop joint interests that brought them together in never-before ways. Such as cooking. It started with John cutting a recipe out of the paper and giving it to Lucy to try. "Why don't you try it?" she said. "What do I know about cooking—why don't we do it together?" he asked. That started them on a pursuit in which they became enthusiastic to the point of obsession and weekends were frequently spent shopping the nearby farm stands for special foods and then converting them into all sorts of unique and exotic dishes which they enjoyed in wine-accompanied candlelight dinners.

John gave up his Sunday golf game in favor of

going off on sorties with Lucy to different golf courses within driving distance, and making a day or even a weekend of it. They began to enjoy each other in new ways, and to rediscover the sort of close companionship that had brought them together thirty-five years ago, but had changed its configuration over the years as the pulls and pressures of career and family building made their inroads.

They also made structural changes in their house to suit their new lifestyle. "What do we need this family room for?" asked John one day. "Let's make it into an exercise room so we can get that Universal equipment and that rowing machine you like."

"While we're about it," said Lucy, "Timmy's old room would make a great study/office for you. We can break right through the living room wall." And they embarked enthusiastically upon the project of redesigning their home for their needs alone, which involved redoing the kitchen to accommodate their new interest in cooking and screening in the back patio so they could enjoy late night suppers on summer evenings instead of the old fast barbecues that had taken place no later than 6 o'clock to accommodate the children's various evening activities.

On their visits home these days, the children professed to be pleased to see their parents so happily engaged, but in fact, they were dismayed to see the changes in their home. "I feel disenfranchised," said Timmy when he saw the conversion of his old room. "Don't worry about it," said John to Lucy when she became concerned that perhaps they made a mistake. "If it were up to the kids, we and the house would be frozen in time. That's how kids are. They're selfish, but we have our lives to live now and they have theirs."

As the years went on, Lucy and John began to resent their children's intrusions. The assumption that they could drop in whenever they wanted, or drop off their children when it suited them became a source of ongoing irritation. Lucy and John were doting grandparents, but on their own terms. Previous generations of grandparents "lived for their grandchildren" as I heard frequently from my mother-in-law who sat home just waiting to be called to either baby sit in my home or have her grandchild in hers. But today grandparents not only don't look like grandparents, they don't act like them either. They're younger in spirit and physical condition than the fifty- and sixty-year-olds of yore, and they are busy, involved people who do not care to live a derivative existence based on their offspring. They resist being imposed upon by their children.

"We served our time. Now we want to enjoy being just us."

I heard that view expressed by many of the "empty nesters" whose children were grown, married, living independently and I realized that the epithet carries an implicit negativism that is inappropriate. The picture of the sad old couple rocking on the porch of the abandoned homestead, once filled with the sounds of frolicking children and now gloomy and silent, is strictly of the past. No longer is mother the pathetic lost individual whose busy flour-covered hands now lie idle and father the worn-out old man with nothing to do but watch the grass grow. The more likely location for this couple today is the golf course or tennis court. And chances are they look upon this time in their lives as a beginning rather than an ending.

This is the era of total freedom. The kids are

grown and gone and no longer demanding of your time and support. You are free of the fiscal and physical responsibilities of their care and maintenance. You're back to square one, the newlywed days of your marriage, only it's better now because you have a marvelous kind of oneness based on a life of shared pains and pleasures. Sex may not have the same level of passion, but it can be just as satisfactory, especially since the partners are now at ease and relaxed and no longer bring to the bedroom those daily anxieties that diminish desire. And the complete privacy in the home frequently brings about a delicious sense of wanton abandon that brings new excitement to their sex relations.

"We both run around the house now stark naked if we feel like it," said one man. "It's marvelous, the freedom and privacy like when we were first married. Do you know how many times in our married life our sex was interrupted by a kid banging on the door for something or other, or a phone call asking to be picked up somewhere? Or how many times we were so exhausted, or aggravated, or upset that weeks and weeks passed without our touching each other? I don't say I'm the same tiger I was years ago, but when the desire is there, we now take the time to arouse each other. And it's great."

Work Less & Play More

Now is the time to have the best of all worlds; decelerate your work load and accelerate your fun load. You've heard the expression, "He's slowed down a bit." The couples I met who altered the ratios of their work and play had hardly slowed down. In fact, if anything they had increased their activities, but were now expending more energy in the pleasure rather than the work areas. Being more secure financially, they were able to adjust their work schedules to allow themselves the pleasures of retirement without the problems brought on by total idleness. Many purchased residences in the South where they spent the winter months, "So we could escape the cold and the kids," one explained with a smile. "When we come back home, we're refreshed and ready to take on our work and the problems our children like to dump on us." That particular couple had two daughters who were divorced and had two children each.

The Problem of the Returning Child

Elise and Len were rarely home any more. A highly esteemed orthodontist with two books and many professional articles to his credit, Len was continually asked to address dental meetings all over the world. Elise, who was a writer, was able to accompany him on his trips and they enjoyed the travel immensely. Now in their early fifties, with two married children, they had created for themselves the kind of idyllic free existence that can be achieved with maturity and money. A house at the beach, a condominium in Florida, a house in the suburbs and the time and wherewithal to enjoy it all. They loved each other, liked being together and revelled in the renewed companionship that had taken a hiatus during the hectic years of child rearing. And then came the fateful phone call.

"Hi, Mom. This is Diane. Ralph just left me, and

we're getting a divorce. I'm so miserable. Can I come home with the kids?"

"Of course, darling. Oh, I'm so sorry," said Elise. Then she had an afterthought. "You mean just for a visit, of course."

"No, Mom—I mean for good. I won't be able to maintain our house, so I'll have to get a job and I have to have somewhere to leave the kids and someone to take care of them. I figured you have that whole floor upstairs that no one is using."

Elise was stunned. "Come, of course. We'll talk about it when you get here."

She hung up the phone in shock. Len walked into the room at that moment and was alarmed by the look on her face.

"What happened?"

She told him. His first reaction was to be upset for his daughter and grandchildren and for the difficult times that surely lay ahead for all of them. And then the full impact of what this could mean to him struck.

"What does she mean move in here—and we take care of her kids? We took care of our children and it's her job to take care of hers. We're not babysitters. I lived through years of crying babies and sleepless nights and worrying about kids who aren't home yet with the car, and I don't plan to do it again. Seems to me this is all her problem, not ours."

"How can we say that, Len? She's our daughter and she's in trouble. We have to help her."

Len said evenly, "Do you want her moving in here disrupting our lives? Do you want to stay home and take care of the kids next month when I go to give that lecture in Paris? And if we want to go to the beach house Wednesday, do you want not to be able to because Kimmy has school which means we can only go Friday afternoon when the traffic is bumper-to-bumper?"

Elise looked miserable. "Oh why didn't I listen to you when you wanted to sell this house and take an apartment in the city? How can we refuse her when we do have the room?"

This kind of problem is coming up with greater frequency as the divorce rate among young couples rises. Years ago, when many generations lived together in large homes, like the Waltons of television fame, family members moved in and out with ease and were always welcome. There was always a parent or grandparent around to mind the little ones, and aunts, uncles and cousins could find a home if they needed one. But the old rambling homestead is a thing of the past and most houses are evaluated by the square foot, and contain two, three or four bedrooms and kitchens that cannot accommodate gatherings of twelve happy Waltons. Today's Grandma is no longer the red-cheeked, biscuit-baking matriarch, nor is Grandpa likely to be the wise, patient patriarch who spends his days teaching the children how to cast a line. Now, once a couple has raised their children, they feel their job is done and they are free to pursue other interests that the readier availability of time and money permits. The return of grown children is regarded as an imposition, and in today's style of mature living, it is.

But what about guilt? How can a parent in good conscience turn down a call for help? After all, when the kids were little, didn't they come crying to you with scraped knees and expect you to make it better? And didn't you? When you took on the role of parents, there was no statute of limitations.

In lower species, once the offspring are weaned and taught how to fend for themselves, they are off on their own forever. But we are of a higher level and maintain a relationship with our children until death do us part. What, oh, what to do?

Len and Elise agonized over the decision about the return of Diane and her children. When she came home, they told her that they would always be there to supply emotional and moral support for her as well as financial help if needed. But they would not take over the job of parenting. They explained that they were not young any more and the physical demands of small children were beyond their capacity. They no longer had the strength or the patience to cope with raising children, and it was unfair of her to expect this of them. If, once her divorce was settled, the alimony and child care payments could not cover maintenance of her house, they would help financially to tide her over until she found a smaller house. What they were telling their daughter essentially was that she would always have the backup of their love and supportiveness as when she was a child, but they could no longer take responsibility for her life. Like all adults, she had to make choices and decisions on her own.

Painful as it was, it turned out to be the right decision. Diane got a good job that enabled her to maintain her house. She found a student at a nearby university who was happy to take over child care in exchange for room and board. She began to construct a new life for herself, which probably would not have happened had she returned to the womb of her parents' home.

When He Retires & She Doesn't

"I enjoy working, it's stimulating. And I just started fifteen years ago. I'm not tired of it, I love it," said a woman whose sixty-two-year-old husband had retired from his job three months earlier.

Her husband thought the whole arrangement was wonderful.

"It's the first time in thirty-five years that I can stay in bed and wave goodbye to my wife."

Sociologists mark it as a striking trend that the labor force participation of older women has grown during the past few decades. In 1950, 27 percent of women between the ages of fifty-five and sixty-four joined the work force, but by 1984 the proportion had risen to 41.7 percent. Paralleling this phenomenon has been the decrease of older men in the marketplace as the increasing availability of pensions and other benefits make retirement attractive, and the new idea that retirement has its own enjoyment style. Yet another reason is the impact of new retirement incentives. According to Dr. William H. Crown, a senior research associate at the Policy Center on Aging at Brandeis University, "Lots of companies have been giving older males the incentive to retire, especially when they were trying to pare down their labor forces during the recession."

For many women, their work may be starting to take off just at the time their husbands are thinking of retirement. The age disparity between many couples also contributes to the gap in their preferred times of retirement.

As one woman said, "I've gotten to like having my own money and being out there in the world. I'd like to work for a few more years at least."

All this makes for some interesting new lifestyles that have become totally acceptable today.

* * *

Dorothy had been a homemaker and mother for the first fifteen years of her marriage to Nate. When the children reached high school age, she took a part-time job with a charitable organization for whom she had been a volunteer worker in previous years. She became more involved with the group and soon was moved up into a full-time employee status and shortly became head of the local branch. During all these years, Nate had been an investment advisor and had supported the family so that Dorothy's earnings were looked upon as "put-away money." As the children grew and went off to college, Dorothy looked for another job and was offered a position as head of a major national organization—a job that entailed heavy responsibilities and a great deal of international and national travel. Since there were no longer any children at home and Nate's work kept him late at the office on many nights, the position seemed ideal for Dorothy. Then when Dorothy was forty-five and Nate fifty-two, he lost his job and suddenly she was the sole breadwinner.

At first, Nate went out looking for another job, but it was difficult to find one at his age and with his specialized background. They discussed it one evening, and Dorothy said: "Look, you supported us for all these years, now maybe it's my turn. My salary could easily pay for our living expenses and even luxuries, and we have investments that you can take care of. It may not be full-time work for you, but what's wrong with taking it easier now? You've put in your time."

At the beginning, the new lifestyle seemed somewhat strange to both of them, with Dorothy going off in the morning and Nate asking her what time she'd be home and what he should do for dinner. She noticed that her attitude toward work was slightly different. The somewhat cavalier attitude she had had before, when she did not regard her working as mandatory, was now gone. There was a little fear there, as she realized she *needed* the job. As she put it, "It's lovely to work when you don't have to. It's tougher to cope when you know you have to."

Nate became used to being the only male spouse on convention trips, where customarily the men were at meetings and the wives were being treated to fashion shows and museum tours. He began to enjoy playing tennis and swimming while Dorothy was locked in conferences all day. "What the hell, that's what she used to do when I went to conventions. Why not me?" Soon, the initial guilt was gone, and he was no longer ashamed to answer the phone during the day. Nor did he mind when people asked him what he did and he said, "Nothing."

When I asked Dorothy when she plans to retire she said, "Not for a long time. To tell you the truth, this life is great. I enjoy my work and all the accolades I get from it, and it's wonderful to come home and find everything ready—my drink, dinner, the works. and a nice guy to spend the evening and night with. I've often heard career women say that what they would like at the end of a day is a wife. They're right."

Retirement . . . Grating & Gratifying

The old saying, "I married him for better or worse but not for lunch," is the feeling that was expressed by almost every woman with a recently retired husband who had not yet adjusted to the new 24-hour togetherness. If the wife continued to work after her spouse retired, everything was fine. He became a "house husband" and, depending upon how he took to the new domestic role, their life continued along smoothly. But if they both gave up their worklives simultaneously, or if she was not employed and he was now a daily participant in her area of responsibility—the home—difficulties arose.

This is the period when the working woman gets the payback for all those rough years of assuming a double role. As mentioned earlier in this book, even though a woman may have a job that is equally demanding as her husband's, it is she who carries the additional onus of running the household. Which means that at retirement time, he is totally idle and out of work, but she still has the raison d'étre of homemaker. Since it's just the two of them, the tasks are not onerous but they have the value of giving purpose and structure to her days. The problem is her husband, who now wanders aimlessly about and usually tries to insinuate himself into her activities.

"Why do you shop at two different stores? You use up too much gas that way and it can't be cost efficient," he will state after doing an informal time-and-motion study of her marketing habits.

"Because one store has the brand of coffee beans

we like and the other carries a better quality of meat," she will answer through clenched teeth.

"Where are you going?" "Who was that on the phone?" Every wife of a retiree told me that these were the sort of daily questions that drove her crazy at first. "He was always there, always around. I never seemed to have the house to myself like I was used to, ever. And he was always looking over my shoulder with suggestions about how to do this and that." Procedures that he formerly took for granted, like vacuuming the carpets, or washing vegetables, now got the benefit of his business efficiency evaluation and his wife was treated to lectures on how to improve on the performance of her household chores.

"He was driving me up the wall," said one woman "until he finally got involved with politics and the city council."

Of course, the only way to handle total retirement is to find new activities and interests. It's the time of life when you can finally do what you want to instead of only what you have to do. It's also the time that you can live wherever you want whenever you want—like warm climate in the winter and cool climate in the summer.

Your Place in the Sun

"The afternoon I saw Charles still in his pajamas looking out the apartment window, and I asked why he wasn't dressed and he answered, 'What for?' I knew we had better move to Florida."

Sylvia and Charles still lived in the large comfortable apartment they had moved into 42 years ago when they were married. They had brought up their two children there but now Charles, who had retired two months ago, was spending most of his time wandering around the rooms and staring aimlessly out of the windows. Charles' total interest had been his job and he was unprepared for the idleness of retirement. Try though she may to get him involved in activities, hobbies and ways to occupy his time, Sylvia could not get a rise out of him. Each day he got up later and later, dressed, ate breakfast, went down for the newspaper and then spent the entire morning reading the first half and the afternoon reading the second half. The rest of the day and evening was dedicated to watching television. It upset her to watch the deterioration of a once-active and vital man into a virtual vegetable. When she saw that one day he did not even have the desire to get dressed, she knew he had reached a nadir and she had better take some steps before he sank into an irreversible depression.

"Charles, let's move to Florida."

"What's in Florida?" he asked.

"For one thing, warm weather so that you could be on the golf course instead of staring out the window at the snow. You said yourself that all our friends are down there. Let's fly down and take a look."

They saw a condominium they liked in Fort Lauderdale, put down a deposit and returned home. Charles looked around the apartment that had been their home for their entire married life and said: "Let's not burn all our bridges behind us and give up this place before we know how we'll like Florida. How about sub-letting this apartment for a year and moving South on a trial basis?"

Their daughter came to help them pack. This did not help their morale since she walked around with tears coursing down her cheeks, muttering things like, "My parents are deserting me. My children are losing their grandparents." When moving day came, both Sylvia and Charles were miserable and afraid. But once settled into their beautiful spanking-new apartment, they began to get into the sybaritic Floridian lifestyle of people who now have the money and time to devote themselves fully to the pursuit of pleasure. In short order Sylvia and Charles joined with their new and old friends revelling in their newly assumed role of jet-setters, their days spent around the pool or golf course discussing investments or planning trips, and evenings devoted to dining in all the best spots in town. Charles became a member of the board of directors of their condominium and was busily devoted to maintaining the luxurious qualities of their building. Sylvia joined the local branches of charitable organizations to which she had belonged previously and they both developed an even wider circle of friends. Even the children had to admit that their parents looked marvelous, and were, after all, accessible by phone and plane. Almost a year later, a tanned, glowing Charles turned to his wife as they sat viewing the Atlantic Ocean from their ninth-story terrace, "What a life! Let's give up the old apartment. What could be better than this?"

In Sickness & in Health

Freedom from financial and familial responsibilities is the good part of the Seventh Level of marriage. But unfortunately, this time of marriage is also when disability can strike.

When a spouse becomes seriously ill unexpectedly—a strong possibility once the couple has passed the age of fifty—life can change radically. This is when all the qualities of love, caring and supportiveness come into use and the true value of a good, successful marriage becomes apparent.

This is a topic on which I did extensive research involuntarily, and the following case history is mine.

David's diabetes was of the adult-onset type that showed up when he was middle-aged. It was controlled with pills and seemed unimportant so we ignored it for years. One day he noticed a sore on his left foot that became angrier and bloodier and refused to heal. Antibiotics did not help. The doctor became alarmed as signs of gangrene were becoming evident, so we called our friend, Joe Ransohoff, the world-famous neurosurgeon, who said, "Bring him down here right away. We have a great vascular surgeon for this kind of stuff . . . let him have a look." We went to the doctor's office at New York University Hospital for what we expected would involve a routine visit expecting to pick up a prescription and return home. I returned home: David remained in the hospital for four months.

The vascular bypass operation required to bring healing blood to the wound took seven hours. It was a success, for a week. I was summoned from the seminar I was teaching at Marquette University in Milwaukee by a phone call from my assistant: "The doctor's office phoned to say they just took David down for more surgery and that's all I know."

I flew back at once and at the hospital learned that the operation had "blown." This meant the new tissues did not hold and the entire bypass had to be redone. The new surgery was fine, for a week, and then it blew again, and it was back to the operating room. When I saw the surgeon immediately afterwards, he looked beat and depressed as he told me that diabetics had endless bacteria floating around in their bodies which makes surgery chancy. David had contracted a severe infection from an unknown virulent strain which not only destroyed the surgery but threatened to destroy his life unless they could identify the bacteria and locate the antidote within days. To make things worse, should they be fortunate enough to cure the infection in time, he would inevitably lose his leg.

I was editor/publisher of *Medical/Mrs.* magazine at that time and David was the art director, which means we were dealing with inescapable deadlines. I worked until four every day and then drove one hour to the hospital where I stayed until eight in the evening and then drove home. I did this for four months. During this period, at first David was in a quarantined glass room which I could enter only after putting on surgical mask, gown and gloves. This would be required until the source of the infection was determined and cured. He was then moved to the intensive care unit where he remained longer than any patient in recent memory. On weekends I stayed at a friend's house nearby so that I could be there at the sporadic visiting hours prescribed for the ICU, starting at 8:00 a.m.

Every hospital patient needs an advocate, someone who loves and cares deeply for his well-being, like a wife or husband. Someone who hollers until a doctor removes the terribly uncomfortable respirator that renders the patient mute and unable to complain. Someone who rips a lamp off the nursing station desk to illuminate the patient's wound for the doctor's examination in a room that was designed stupidly with lights at the head but not foot of the beds. Someone who convinces the dietician of the idiocy of continuing to furnish tasteless but dietetically correct meals to a patient whose weight is dropping rapidly. Someone who finds out where they hide the containers of cold milk that the patient loves but can never seem to get. That someone is generally a husband or wife. In this case, I was that someone.

The longer one stays in a hospital, the greater the risk of developing new difficulties. There was the night when the phone rang at 1:00 a.m. It was David telling me he was being taken back to the ICU because he had spiked a 107° fever and a life-threatening pulmonary embolism was suspected, accurately.

Through all this, my being there every day kept him going and fighting. His face would light up when I entered the room and he told me what a lift it gave him to hear the unmistakable sound of my fast footsteps in the corridor. What he did not know was that my speedy approach was due to my anxiety to see his condition and the dreadful knot in the pit of my stomach caused by fear over what I might find when I entered his room each day.

Our daughter was there constantly; she was finishing law school and trying to study for the bar exam yet managed to be at the hospital almost every day or evening. When David could not attend her graduation, she got special permission from the school to keep her gown and mortarboard an extra day so that she could show herself in full regalia to her proud father in the ICU for whom it was the highlight of his day if not life.

The doctors and nurses marvelled at David's uncomplaining behavior and bravery and at the miracle of a person who was not disoriented by the

24-hour lights-and-action of the ICU which usually distorts patients' perceptions. I attribute his stability to three factors: his deep strength and will to survive, the constancy of his wife and daughter who gave him the desire to live, and his beloved classical music supplied by his radio and the marvelous station WNCN.

I am using myself here only as an example. During the four months, I saw many spouses who devoted themselves to their ill mates. Since statistically men are the weaker sex, most of the patients were husbands. We were all there every day, every night, encouraging our husbands with feigned assurances of ultimate recovery while inwardly we quaked with fear and frequently cried ourselves to sleep at night in our half-empty beds.

One elderly woman whose husband was in a post-operative coma slept for seven days on the hard benches in the ICU waiting room, performing her morning ablutions in the public washroom and depending on friends and family to bring her food while she awaited the moment when her husband might come to, which he never did.

As we watched David's toes turn black and the gangrene creep up his leg daily, we knew the amputation was inevitable. His pain became so intense that he lived from demerol shot to demerol shot. Finally, they did a below-the-knee amputation which leaves a joint that makes it easier to adapt to a prosthesis. We thought the worst was finally over. Then a week later, I was awakened at 2:00 a.m. with a call from David telling me they were taking him back down to the operating room because of hemorrhaging. He then put the surgeon on the phone. "Do I have your permission to amputate above the knee if necessary?" "No," I said immediately. "What are you doing, cutting him away piece by piece?" "I don't want to," he said, "but it may be the only life-saving action I can take or he could bleed to death. If you don't give me permission, it's like sending me to fight a war without weapons." I had no recourse and the second amputation was performed.

Afterwards, David and I tried to maintain a façade of cheer, but there was the afternoon when we looked at the empty space under the sheet where his leg had been and I held him in my arms as we sobbed softly together.

By this time, David had been in the hospital for three months, had undergone seven operations and a pulmonary embolism and now weighed 112 pounds instead of his customary 160. I kept pleading with the doctor to release him. I could take care of him at home, because I feared more hospital-incurred disasters. And then one more occurred. From lying in bed so long, David developed difficulty with his prostate and an operation was necessary. So he had his eighth bout with surgery.

When he recovered from that, and his amputation wound seemed to be healing, the doctor began to entertain the idea of sending him home. "But the dressing on the wound will have to be changed a few times daily, and a visiting nurse can only come in once a day," he told me. "Show me how," I said.

The surgical nurse who I had come to know well looked at me that day and said in amazement "You look marvelous. I don't know how you do it." "I have to now," I said. "I'll have time to fall apart later." She looked at me pityingly. "But you can't. That's when the toughest part begins."

We brought David home in late August, just before his birthday. We all cried with joy that day. He confessed then that he thought he would never see home again and told me that if it weren't for me, he never would have made it. For a number of weeks, I donned a surgical mask and gloves and tended his wound until it healed enough to take him for his first fitting for a prosthesis—an exciting day because, as he put it, "I can be a biped again." Up to that point he had been in a wheelchair. Not that he stayed home. I was determined that our life would be as near normal as possible, so I pushed him in his wheelchair down our front lawn and steps to the car so that we could drive places and to restaurants to have dinner as we used to. Until my daughter insisted we build a ramp or, as she put it, "I'll have two sick parents!"

The first day he was fitted with a temporary prosthesis and walked across the room, we were exhilarated and joyous. He practiced indefatigably to adapt to the new appendage and soon was walking fairly well. He was deservedly proud of his achievement and his old sense of humor returned so that when one helpful passerby saw him struggling to ascend steps, asked, "Can I give you a hand?" David answered, "No thanks, but I can use a leg."

After getting over the natural mourning period for the loss of his limb (and that's exactly what it is), he now became depressed about what he felt was a disfiguring mutilation. David, who was handsome, told me that he was now unattractive. I knew that it was important that he feel I was not repelled, so from that point on I initiated sexual relations, because he could not, until I was able by my actions to make him feel as desirable as before. The next few years were as normal as possible. And then came the next diabetic disaster—his eyes.

His cataract operation was followed by a detached

retina operation and then another operation called a scleral buckle, and he emerged without any close vision. In other words, he could see from the side, but was virtually unable to read or do close work. For a graphic artist who loved to read, this was devastating. In time, with his great strength, he adjusted to this new handicap but hid it from everyone. When we went to restaurants with friends, we played a game, he and I, at menu-reading time. I would read a few selections aloud, as though making my choice, and he would select one. None of our friends was aware that he was almost blind.

Impaired vision made walking difficult for him. We continued to go places, but now we walked tightly arm-in-arm. Fortunately, I work at home so that I could bring him into the business somewhat by coming in periodically to report on the latest happenings and thus make him feel still part of things. And then came the final diabetic punishment—the kidneys. When they started to fail, he sank into a deep depression that I could not counteract. I found a marvelous compassionate psychiatrist, Dr. Edwin Rabiner, who made housecalls. In May, six years after the onset of his troubles and four days before our 35th wedding anniversary, David died. When I had first talked to Dr. Rabiner alone after he had seen David initially, he told me that he had reviewed David's medical condition and that he was a very, very sick man. "I know that," I told him. "We just have to make him the best possible David Smith he can be." And I believe that we did.

The Best Is Last

Like a child who saves his favorite food for the end, I've kept the best for last. This is the story of a marriage that embodies the classic perfection—if such a concept is possible in human relationships—of what marriage can be if the participants are willing to cope with tribulations, some of which have been described in the earlier pages of this book and even some that weren't.

* * *

Perhaps the idea can best be explained in a description of the marriage of the famous pianist Vladimir Horowitz and his wife Wanda as given by a close friend in a story in *Time* magazine:

"I think that the Horowitzes have a relationship that transcends most marriages. They have suffered, they have been hurt, and they have come through with a degree of happiness that is freer and better than anything they had before."

The couple I am going to describe have just that kind of relationship after forty years of marriage—in which there was plenty of tough sledding along the way.

Glenda and Leon were married when she was twenty and he was forty years old, a disparity in age that caused a spate of warnings from friends about the inevitable difficulties that would arise and the almost certain ultimate failure of the union. Given the multi-generational gap and other differences, such as the fact that she was an unsophisticated girl still living at home with her parents while he was an established professional who had been married and divorced, plus the added complication of a nine-year-old son who lived with him, dire predictions did not seem unrealistic. But they were very much in love and each felt they did not want to live without the other, and since nothing in life is guaranteed, they were married.

The first two years were horrific for Glenda. Totally inexperienced and unsure of herself, she moved into an established home replete with resident housekeeper who had been caring for the child. Thus, the burden was apparently upon her to fit into the routine of the household.

As she looks back upon those early days, she says sadly:

"I never had the fun of setting up house like most young couples, or even furnishing a room. Everything was there and I had to just move into it. It would have been so nice to get new things together, to shop and pick out things we both liked. But there it was and I had to adjust."

And adjust is what *she* did. Almost all of the couples interviewed admitted that in the early years of their marriages, 90 percent of the compromising was done by the wives. Women are trained from childhood that the way to get your way with men is to be submissive and accommodating, thereby trapping them into doing things they really want to do but are too obtuse to perceive. We are taught to flatter, listen, and snare because marriage is something we dream of from girlhood (ever see a girl doodling her initials together with that of her current crush to see how the towel monograms would look?) and boys rarely think about. Even in current days, with women being independent and liberated, the process continues. In the Woody Allen movie *Hannah and Her Sisters* there is a scene where two attractive women are being driven around New York by a handsome architect who is blithely pointing out the sights while the two passengers are falling over themselves to flatter, please and get his attention. It's demeaning and it's demanding, but women regard the ritual as worth the investment. If that's what it takes to get married, if a certain amount of dissembling and restraint is required to coerce him into a happy family life that both will enjoy and find fulfilling, then so be it.

This is just how Glenda felt. But the pains were plentiful. Leon was a highly organized and obsessive person who had a routine that had to be followed or there would be hell to pay like the day he chastised her for not arranging the soda bottles in the refrigerator in order of usage:

"You know we use more club soda than ginger ale. Then why put the ginger ale in front?"

If Glenda were more self-assured, she would have laughed at many of his directives and told him to bug off, but her feelings of inadequacy made her accept all criticism as justified. She lived with the fear of being compared unfavorably to his former wife and the sense of being expendable at any time.

"I took crap like no young woman today would," she said. "When I think back to the way I thought everything Leon said was right and I must be wrong, I can't believe it. But what did I know? I felt I was just a kid and he knew everything. Even when it came to buying the house."

After two years, their daughter was born and now, with two youngsters, Leon decided they needed a house in the suburbs. Someone told him about an old house that needed work but was in a nice area and would go for an excellent price. He looked at it and came home to tell Glenda that he had bought them a house. When he took her to see it, she was horribly disappointed. She had so looked forward to finally having the chance to pick out something that would be spanking new and hers alone, but her husband assured her that this was a terrific buy and that was that.

They moved in and Glenda spent six grueling months living amidst carpenters, painters and plumbers while she ran a household with two young children and a husband who had to be driven to and from the railroad station. But the house did get finished and turned into just what Leon had said—a nice house in a nice neighborhood and a fine place to bring up children and settle into the good life.

Now what was Glenda getting from all this during these seemingly punitive years? It would appear that she was doing all the giving. But there were many rewards that, although not immediately apparent, were vital to her. Earlier I talked about marriage being the satisfaction of needs. Glenda was a highly intelligent and sensitive person with a strong desire for upward mobility who grew up in a home totally devoid of niceties, where life was met on a functional basis of nurturing the body but never the soul.

She had an older sister who got all the new clothes, which, when outgrown, were then done over for Glenda. No one paid heed to the natural craving of a pretty little girl to have something of her own that was new. Her parents, who had a retail store, sent her to make deliveries to the homes of her schoolmates without any awareness of the embarrassment this caused to a sensitive child.

Given this background, it is easy to see how important it was for Glenda to have nice clothes, a luxurious home and a standard of living higher than she had experienced as a child. Her marriage to Leon brought her all that, and she revelled in her status as the wife of a respected and well-to-do professional living in an upscale suburb. Not only did she love her life, but she loved and respected her husband deeply. Equally important, he who initially regarded her as somewhat of an inexperienced youngster who required guidance, developed a tremendous respect for her capability and judgment, and his love and need for her grew enormously day by day.

What happened between them is exactly as described in the chapter on the Acceptance Level, where each one's preferences subconsciously became the major considerations in the partner's decision-making mechanism.

Glenda had learned what made her husband happy, so it became routine to do things in that way. She aligned the soda bottles in the refrigerator in order of usage without even thinking about it. And as she made life easy and pleasurable for him, his love and dependency increased, which was very gratifying to her. After many years of doing things to please each other, which one's personal preference initiated the activity was forgotten and their tastes became identical. They both loved to travel, to go to the movies and to theater and dinner. In fact, they decided that staying at home was destructive for them and would turn them into couch potatoes, so they kept moving and went out five nights out of seven. They were perfect examples of the marital pleasure of doing things a spouse enjoys for the pure satisfaction of sharing his or her delight and then growing to love the activity equally.

Of course, they endured the usual troubles one can expect during many years of marriage. Periods of financial difficulty, and problems with children that were the source of strong conflicts and emotional confrontations. But they weathered them, and the tribulations strengthened their bond.

When I talked to them in their lovely new home (oh, yes, they moved from the first house after the children were grown and were now in a house they both had chosen and Glenda finally had the chance to furnish together with Leon), they were the picture of contentment. Here was a man eighty years old who looked twenty years younger and had the vitality and energy that would tire a thirty-year-old. The affection and love between them was palpable and they kept reaching for each other's hand as some remembered incident triggered a smile. At the conclusion of our meeting, Glenda looked at her husband fondly and turned to me and said:

"Maybe the first ten years were hell—but the next thirty were well worth it."

Conclusion: Why I Loved Being married, They Loved Being Married, You'll Love Being Married

The way I see it, sharing your way through life with someone you love is the only way to go. It makes hard times more bearable and good times richer.

There is no great mystique to a successful marriage, although it is symptomatic of the current quick-solution-mentality that serves up microwaves and McDonalds for fast foods and computers for instant results to demand a simple formula for the creation of a happy union.

A few years ago I was on a trip with a group of young journalists in their thirties. At the end of the junket, during our farewell celebration, one of the women asked me how long I had been married. When I told her thirty years, her eyes opened incredulously. "My God," she said, "What's the secret?"

I told her, as I am telling you, there is no single panacea or prescribed process that assures a smooth path through the life of a marital relationship. It is a blending of elements, and it takes place over a protracted period of time. If you marry with the unrealistic expectations that your partner will accede to your desires because of love alone and that happiness will be instantaneous, you're in for trouble. For one thing, what is happiness? I once asked my eighty-five-year-old mother-in-law if she was happy. "Happy?" she said. "What's happy? I'm content." None of us could endure a steady life diet of parties, dress-ups and fancy foods. For life to be interesting, we must also have the commonplace, the quiet times, even the difficulties. Real companionship is not dependent upon scintillating conversation and stimulating escapades as in the old Cary Grant movies, but upon the enjoyment of sharing experiences that matter.

Marriage is simply a way of life. "How well an individual understands himself and his own personality needs, and how well he habitually gets along with himself and with others will have much to do with the success of his marriage. Marriage does not change basic personality. Sometimes people marry with the expectation that marriage will work miracles in their lives, that it will bring them happiness when they lack the habit of happiness, and that it will resolve all their maladjustments. That is expecting too much of marriage. Those who marry with an intelligent understanding of their own marriageability and an appreciation of their obligations as well as their privileges are likely to achieve great success and happiness."*

One of the major pre-marital misconceptions that is bound to cause trouble is that you will change your mate after marriage. Your spouse will not become a different person; all that will alter are his loyalties and responses to you. Before I was married, a whole string of friends warned me that my husband-to-be was too attached to his mother and aunt to the point of dangerous psychosis. Actually what happened after marriage was that all the love and affection that had been directed to them was, in time, shifted to me. But I did not have the unrealistic expectations that this would happen overnight.

A piece of legal paper cannot change a person's emotions instantly. If I had been foolish enough to demand that he make an immediate choice between me and his family, I would have lost. He needed the love and emotional support they had given him all his life, and he responded to that with deep gratitude and attachment. In time, as we lived together and built a happy life, his loyalties naturally shifted as he now depended upon me to provide the soul-nurturing sustenance previously provided by them, and his relationship to his family settled into normalcy. So much for the armchair psychologists who had predicted the demise of my marriage within one year. Included in those doubters was my mother, who I later learned had told my maid-of-honor before the ceremony that she did not expect the marriage to last, but at least "Cynthia will have one

*Judson T. and Mary G. Landis, *Building a Successful Marriage*, Englewood Cliffs, NJ: Prentice-Hall, Inc., 1953.

nice wedding." My thirtieth-anniversary-party invitations read: "Come and celebrate our thirtieth (and my mother said it would never last!)"

It's all a question of attitude and expectation. Don't lay down big rules that are bound to be broken. Don't set up a stiff set of stipulations that are sure to fail. Just let it all happen and take things one day at a time. And above all, do not look upon the marital relationship as an onerous project that must be handled.

On a recent Phil Donahue TV show, I heard a number of young marrieds state with solemnity the need to "work at a marriage." If ever there was a turnoff term, that is it. "Work" according to the dictionary means toil and labor, with synonyms given as drudgery and travail. The very word is a downer. You don't "work" at marriage any more than you "work" at crossing the street when you must look in either direction, or "work" at getting dressed in the morning when you must select the blouse or shirt that goes with the suit. You just do it the way you do everything—by learning, reacting and making choices and decisions. It's the same thing with a marriage. You just go about the business of living and respond instinctually without giving conscious thought to every move. If you systematically analyze every act you performed daily, you would be worn out in a week.

But this all takes TIME.

And you don't expect miracles.

A woman I know complained about her new husband's lack of appreciation for her culinary talents, which she regarded as considerable. She had divorced a gentle, lovely man because he did not provide her with the wealth she craved and married a very rich man who furnished lavish monetary but little emotional support. "Peter used to praise my cooking all the time. He really appreciated me," she said mournfully, recalling the nice qualities of her former husband.

"Lillian," I said, "marriage is not a Chinese meal. You can't choose one from Group A and one from Group B. You take each package complete, as it comes."

I have heard many young people make similar plaintive comparisons between their spouses and former girlfriends and boyfriends. "He's great when it comes to this, but lousy when it comes to that." When you are tempted to make the same sort of remarks, remember that no one, including you, can be all things to all people at all times. If, on balance, you are getting fulfillment of your vital key needs, then just overlook the rest. As times goes on, these petty annoyances will diminish in importance and become something we all have to deal with, like traffic tieups and taxes.

A forty-six-year-old man I know told me recently that he had never married because he hadn't yet met anyone with whom he wanted to spend his entire life. What he didn't realize was that though love at first sight may be charming, marriage at first sight is ridiculous. You don't meet someone and say, "Wow, I want to be with this person 24-hours a day forever!" And you don't start out by evaluating and judging. You just let the relationship develop until you arrive at the feeling of pleasure in being together that tells you that this can be the basis of a marriage that will grow in depth as you share small as well as big experiences. And then you take the plunge.

If you are newly married and wonder how you will ever make it, just look around the way I did when I was struggling to learn how to drive a car. When I saw all the thousands of people of various economic, ethnic and educational levels driving, then I realized that I could do it, too. Most of the world is married and probably went through much the same adjustment hassles as you.

But when you see that special intimacy, understanding and love that shines forth from couples who have been happily married for many years, you realize that this is an incomparable and priceless relationship that comes only with time and caring, and, once achieved, will become the essence of your life.

There will be plenty of times when you will say, "What do I need this for? Is it worth it?" Just keep on remembering, "Yes, it sure as hell is." And think of the many things in your life that took effort but which you did unquestioningly because you knew that the payoff warranted the investment.

A young woman who had been married for five years told me that she loved her husband but they were "having problems." Who doesn't? Of course, there can be insurmountable difficulties that arise where divorce is the only solution, but when we discussed the nature of the problems, they involved her husband's unwillingness to talk things out. As it turned out, it was not unwillingness as much as inability. Most women are better able than men to talk intimately about themselves. Also, both sexes have been socialized to see relationship-maintenance as primarily a woman's responsibility, so men rarely learn how to approach the subject.

This woman must learn to recognize that he is unprepared, unfamiliar and uncomfortable with the kinds of talk she demands. Her acceptance may not necessarily eliminate feelings of frustration and irritation, and she may holler or turn silent, depending on how she handles anger. But in what area of your life do you get everything you want?

When I interviewed couples who had been happily married for more than fifteen years, the total contentment with their situation was absolute, but every single one mentioned that, of course, they had problems along the way. Each person develops a tolerance for the other's drawbacks and this understanding just becomes another element to be woven into the fabric of their joint existence.

Judson and Mary Landis offer this definition: "A successful marriage is one in which two people have intelligently committed themselves to a lifetime together, in which each seeks to enrich the life of the other as well as his own. In a successful marriage each partner, because of the marriage, stands as a more integrated person, better able to meet and cope adequately with the vicissitudes of life. Such a marriage is based on cooperation and includes the most rewarding comradeship. In a good marriage each partner is all that he himself is capable of being; moreover, his personality expands and takes on, in a measure, the attributes and capacities of the partner. Both are conscious that an interdependence exists by which the two stand together, so that pleasures are enhanced through the sharing, and blows which life may offer are cushioned."*

I was married to the same man for almost thirty-five years. We had our rough stretches, moments when anger made us wonder if the love had disappeared from the relationship. But when one takes the time to allow the furies to subside, the love resurfaces if you give it the chance.

*Ibid., p. 2.

The aim of this book is to convince you to always give your marriage the chance to succeed. It is an ongoing process of weighing and waiting. There is no specific point where the relationship is invulnerable, and the danger only comes when the partners respond precipitously instead of propitiously to a problem. Sometimes a situation may seem intolerable, but you may only be going through a phase of your level of marriage and can take comfort in knowing that it will pass as it has for others.

When you observe that special self-confidence and contentment emanated by couples who are sure of their love for each other and enjoy the sense of security that comes from knowing there's always someone there for them, and the greater pleasure produced by sharing experiences, you realize that a happy marriage is the most nurturing and satisfactory of all human relationships. It is not a rarified state, it is a reachable state. All you have to do is reach for it.

Bibliography

Gould, Roger L. *Transformations: Growth and Change in Adult Life,* New York: Simon and Schuster, 1978.

Jung, Carl G. *Modern Man in Search of a Soul,* Boston: Harcourt Brace, 1939.

Klagsbrun, Francine. *Married People,* New York: Bantam Books, 1985

Landis, Judson T. and Mary G. *Building a Successful Marriage,* Englewood Cliffs, NJ, 1953.

Masters, William H. et al. *The Pleasure Bond: A New Look at Sexuality and Commitment,* Boston: Little Brown and Company, 1975.

Pietropinto, Anthony and Jacqueline Simenauer. *Husbands and Wives: A Nationwide Survey of Marriage,* New York: Times Books, 1979.

Sheehy, Gail. *Passages,* New York: Bantam Books, 1977.

About The Author

CYNTHIA S. SMITH is the author of three books, among them *Doctors' Wives: The Truth About Medical Marriages*. She Was editor and publisher of *Medical/Mrs.*, a magazine for doctors' wives, and has been on the Phil Donahue Show, the *Today* show, and many other TV programs. She lectures throughout the U.S. and has given seminars at 42 universities. Formerly on the faculties of New York University and the University of Connecticut, she is also president of her own advertising agency. She has a daughter, Hillary, and lives in a glass house in Rye, New York.